CHARLES T. TART

NEW THINKING ALLOWED DIALOGUES

Charles T. Tart
Seventy Years of Exploring Consciousness and Parapsychology

JEFFREY MISHLOVE

www.whitecrowbooks.com

Charles T. Tart.

Copyright © 2025 by New Thinking Allowed Foundation. All rights reserved.
Published by New Thinking Allowed, an imprint of White Crow Productions Ltd.

The right of Jeffrey Mishlove to be identified as the author of this work has been
asserted by him in accordance with the Copyright, Design and Patents act 1988.

A CIP catalogue record for this book is available from the British Library.
For information, contact White Crow Books by e-mail: info@whitecrowbooks.com.

Cover Design by Jana Rogge & Astrid@Astridpaints.com
Interior design by Velin@Perseus-Design.com

Paperback: ISBN: 9781786772763
eBook: ISBN: 9781786772770

Non Fiction / Body, Mind & Spirit / Parapsychology /
ESP, Clairvoyance, Precognition, Telepathy.

www.whitecrowbooks.com

Charles T. Tart

Acknowledgments

~

The New Thinking Allowed Foundation is a nonprofit organization dedicated to fostering greater awareness in the areas of philosophy, psychology, health, science, and spirituality—with an emphasis on parapsychology and the paranormal. The activities of the Foundation include the *New Thinking Allowed* channel on YouTube, as well as the publication of a weekly email Newsletter and a Magazine, in addition to the *New Thinking Allowed Dialogues* book series. Visit our website at newthinkingallowed.org.

We are staffed almost entirely by volunteers. Special thanks are due to Elizabeth Lord, Laura Neubert, and Emmy Vadnais for their assistance in the preparation of this book.

Special thanks are also due to Jon Beecher, publisher of White Crow Books.

Books Authored by Charles T. Tart:

Altered states of consciousness (1969)
On Being Stoned: A Psychological Study of Marijuana Intoxication (1971)
States of Consciousness (1975)
Transpersonal Psychologies: Perspectives on the Mind from Seven Great Spiritual Traditions (1975)
Symposium on Consciousness (1975, with co-authors)
Learning to Use Extrasensory Perception (1976)
Psi: Scientific Studies of the Psychic Realm (1977)
Mind at Large: Institute of Electrical and Electronic Engineers Symposia on the Nature of Extrasensory Perception (1979, co-edited with Harold E. Puthoff and Russell Targ).
Waking Up: Overcoming the Obstacles to Human Potential (1986)
Open Mind, Discriminating Mind: Reflections on Human Possibilities (1989)
Living the Mindful Life: A Handbook for Living in the Present Moment (1994)
Body Mind Spirit: Exploring the Parapsychology of Spirituality (1997)
Mind Science: Meditation Training for Practical People (2001)
The End of Materialism: How Evidence of the Paranormal Is Bringing Science and Spirit Together (2009)

CONTENTS

~

A Note from Jeff

~

I have known Professor Charles T. Tart (1937 – 2025) for over a half-century. Throughout that entire time, he has been recognized as a leading light in both psychology and parapsychology. He has been an inspiration to uncountable thousands of people. The last time my wife, Janelle, and I visited Charley, at his home in Berkeley, he was just turning 87 and not in the best of health. His last breath was on March 5, 2025. My world has lost one of its brightest stars. I owe Charley a considerable debt of gratitude. Let me explain why.

In 1973, I embarked upon an unusual academic adventure. After receiving a Master of Criminology degree from the University of California, Berkeley, I decided to switch fields. Taking advantage of an obscure rule of the Graduate Division, I created an interdisciplinary doctoral program in parapsychology, of which I was the sole student. To do so, I was required to enlist the support of at least three faculty members from the vast University of California system who would be willing to guide my program.

I enlisted the support of C. West Churchman, a business professor and systems theorist. Additionally, the renowned educational evaluator and philosopher of science, Michael Scriven, agreed to become my dissertation supervisor. Most importantly, I secured the support and guidance of Charles T. Tart who was an active parapsychologist and specialist in the study of altered states of consciousness.

The 1970s were a very heady time for parapsychology in the San Francisco Bay Area. Experiments conducted with the Israeli psychic, Uri Geller, at the Stanford Research Institute (now known as SRI International) were being covered by the international press. News was already also leaking out concerning the successful experiments in remote viewing. It seemed, then, as if we were on the cusp of a scientific revolution. In fact, we were then, and we still are now.

In retrospect, I can see I was very idealistic and naïve. I had little appreciation for the strength of the opposition. However, I soon learned that the closer I came to matriculating with the world's first doctoral diploma that stated "Parapsychology" as the single field of study, the more obstacles were placed in my path. There was a professor of statistics who, initially, reached out to me in a supportive tone. Later, however, he revealed himself to be, in his own words, "a hatchet man," whose job was to see that I never graduated. Charley stood by me. Thankfully, we were able to overcome this assault against academic integrity.

Later, there was a Graduate Division Dean who tried to revoke my degree after it had been awarded in 1980, claiming, "Major universities do not award degrees in parapsychology." A campaign was being launched by prominent figures outside of the university to, essentially, destroy my reputation. I ended up fighting a libel suit for six years.

Looking back upon this period of turmoil and stress, I realize that it was the major living nightmare of my life. It affected my sense of well-being and my health. At the end of the day, good people came to my support and, together, we prevailed against these obstacles and threats. Throughout this period of high academic drama, Charley Tart was among my closest advisors and supporters. He was on the inside of this situation and saw exactly what was going on. I can honestly say that he understood, and even felt, the pain I was enduring.

The sixteen interviews presented herein testify to the fact that throughout the decades, Charley and I have remained close. There is no doubt that he has been a major influence on my own thinking. Furthermore, he has been a supporter of my work as an interviewer on topics related to parapsychology and consciousness. At one point, for example, he provided funds to the Vipassana meditation teacher, Shinzen Young, to travel to San Francisco for a series of interviews on the original *Thinking Allowed* television series. On another occasion, he donated signed copies of his classic anthology, *Altered States of Consciousness* as a fundraiser for the *New Thinking Allowed* channel.

A particularly memorable experience occurred on November 8, 2016, when Charley was a guest in our home, then in Las Vegas, NV, on the evening of the shocking presidential election. That was the occasion when ten of the interviews in this book were recorded.

A Note from Jeff

Last year, Charley reached out to me to let me know he was in poor health. Our book of interviews with Russell Targ had just been published; and Charley suggested that, if we were considering doing a similar book featuring my interviews with him, it would be good to get started right away, because he didn't know how much longer he would be around. As you now know, we did do that. I'm so grateful that Charley was able to see the completed manuscript, and cover, before he passed.

My last conversation with Charley was three days before he left this earthly plane. He knew that he was very close to death then, and we had a brief conversation about after-death communication. In fact, just the week before, he had been in the hospital. He would have died then, I think, but they used electroshock to revive him. He made a point of telling me that he did not have a near-death experience on that occasion.

But he knew that his heart was weakened and that he had atrial fibrillation. He didn't believe that he would be able to survive another similar trauma. Nor did he wish to be revived once more.

Charley lived a very full life. He has been a teacher, mentor, and supporter of my work for the past half-century. He put such terms as "altered states" and "state-specific science" into our vocabulary. His research was even spoken about, by actor, William Hurt, in the movie *Altered States*.

Throughout the decades, Charley has been a consistent source of wisdom and guidance. He has been a phenomenal teacher able to discuss transcendental matters in a soft and down-to-earth manner. As a student of spirituality, himself, Charley has practiced various disciplines, ranging from Aikido to the Gurdjieff work. I can testify, based on decades of friendship, that—for me—he is the embodiment not only of knowledge and wisdom, but of compassion.

Foreword[1]

~

Charles Tart: A Noetic Pilgrim's Progress

Etzel Cardeña, PhD.,
Thorsen Professor of Psychology, Lund University

Charles Theodore Tart has been a central figure in the study of altered states of consciousness (ASC), transpersonal psychology, and parapsychology for more than half a century, shifting from mostly being a researcher and theoretician during the first decades to also becoming a pedagogic thinker later. His vast output includes books, articles, and this important series of interviews. In a previous homage, I compared him to an agile hummingbird who pollinated various fields of study that had mostly been left bereft since the towering contributions of William James, who mapped the development of a comprehensive study of the mind, a goal discarded by behaviorism. These 16 interviews by Jeffrey Mishlove represent the breadth of interests and preoccupations of Tart. They include, among other topics, the impact of the characteristics of the experimenter and the experimental setting, the unquestioning allegiances to one or another position about consciousness and reality, the relation (mostly conflictual to him) of science and religion, the differential benefits of different states of consciousness, the relevance of some of the teachings of the esoteric guru Gurdjieff, and how to initiate a meditation practice.

---

[1] This foreword is partly based on Cardeña (2023).

Charles T. Tart.

Tart and Altered States of Consciousness

A whole generation in the 60s, 70s, and 80s encountered a cornucopia of new possibilities to explore changes in consciousness, including visiting the Esalen center to take courses on human potentials, ingesting psychedelics, or starting a then-mysterious practice of meditation. The potential positive or negative outcomes of such adventures were covered, often in sensationalistic and uninformed ways, in newspaper headlines and the TV news, as well as in movies like *Altered States* (1980) by the brilliant director Ken Russell, in which Tart and others were mentioned. Academic books such as Robert Ornstein's *The Nature of Human Consciousness* (1973) and Charles Tart's epoch-making anthology *Altered States of Consciousness* (1969) became bestsellers and textbooks for courses in psychology. Ornstein's 41-chapters book (with two chapters by Tart) criticized a narrow, semi-rational view of science and consciousness, proposing instead "two modes of consciousness" (partly based on research on the two brain hemispheres) and encouraging meditation and Sufism. Tart's book reprinted various scientific articles including an all-encompassing discussion of altered state by Ludwig (1966), and papers on the hypnagogic state, dreaming, meditation, hypnosis, psychedelic drugs, and the psychophysiology of some altered states.

Although Tart's anthology has been by far his most influential book, in my view his most valuable book was *States of Consciousness,* masterfully covering the literature and presenting a system view of how to consider and induce ASC (Tart, 1975a). In my work as editor of two journals on consciousness (*Journal of Anomalous Experience and Cognition* and *Psychology of Consciousness)* and reviewer for other journals, I deplore coming across many papers about ASC that confuse concepts, disregard individual differences, and exhibit other mistakes that had been already clarified in Tart's book.

Besides the books mentioned, Tart conducted many landmark studies, among them a phenomenological study of marijuana intoxication (Tart, 1971); a proposal to create state-specific sciences, published in the bastion journal of mainstream science, *Science* (Tart, 1972); studies of out-of-body-experiences (e. g., Tart, 1998); and studies on dreaming, lucid dreaming, mindfulness, and meditation.[2] Particularly important

---

[2] See https://blog.paradigm-sys.com for a list and description of many of his works.

6

for me were his early studies on transpersonal experiences during deep hypnosis (e.g., Tart, 1970), which inspired my doctoral work and other studies (e. g., Cardeña, 2005; Cardeña et al., 2013).

Tart: Transpersonal Psychology, and Parapsychology

In its official definitions, Transpersonal Psychology has emphasized alterations of consciousness, particularly those in which people experience themselves as part of a larger whole, and initially prioritized empirical research, although that emphasis was lost later (Cardeña, in press). Tart was perhaps the foremost researcher of this movement, partly launching it through another important anthology, *Transpersonal Psychologies* (Tart, 1975b). Cunningham (2023) discusses what he considers Tart's six most important goals for Transpersonal Psychology:

- developing a psychology of mind and spirit
- a critical view of mainstream reductive materialist psychology and its implications,
- adopting an empirical, non-dogmatic approach to religions as spiritual psychologies,
- creating a state-specific science of extraordinary human experience
- grounded in the scientific foundation of experimental parapsychology
- and developing a psychology to assist human growth.

This list, to a large degree, provides a roadmap for the various interviews in this book. I discuss now the fifth point within the context of Tart's contributions to parapsychology (psi). A major thrust of his approach has been to empirically investigate extraordinary claims related to ASC and anomalous experiences, such as out-of-body experiences in which people experience observing from high above their bodies. He mentions in the interviews studies he carried out with two people who could regularly induce such experiences (e.g., Tart, 1998) and proposes that we have to investigate the consensual validity of such claims rather than automatically dismissing (as is wont from a "scientist" perspective) or accepting (as some experients do) them, distinguishing between anomalous experiences and events (Cardeña et al., 2014). Although not all or probably even most such experiences can offer measurable evidence, a relevant finding is that surveys and controlled psi experiments have found a relation between experiencing alterations of consciousness and being successful in psi tasks (e.g., Cardeña & Marcusson-Clavertz, 2020).

Two other major contributions of Tart to parapsychology include his collaboration with Russell Targ and Harold Puthoff in the development of remote viewing (RV). His own striking RV example reminded me of an anecdote of my own, in which Elisabeth Targ (the late daughter of Russell Targ) led me through an associative remote viewing session to try to predict a job outcome. My imagery and related drawing matched very well the target for the desired future event, although that event did not come to pass.

Another important contribution was the application of learning theory, particularly the importance of feedback, during psi experiments. In one of the interviews, Tart describes how he invented two machines (he mentions his technological experience and know-how) to test his theory about feedback. His is still a valid proposal although I think that his complaint about other researchers in the field not investigating it further has more to do with investigators generally wanting to advance their pet theories than someone else's.

All Roads Lead to (Altering) Consciousness

At the end of the road of this foreword, I spell out a few similarities and differences in how Tart and I arrived at our interest and understanding of ASC and related issues. We share a few things: a very religious grandmother, although his cast a much larger, loving shadow on his life. Like he, I was also homebound for a couple of months because of rheumatic fever.

The background differences, though, are more noticeable. He was brought up in a U. S. household with, I surmise, not much influence from his parents, about whom he mentions very little in the interviews. From an earlier age he was interested in electronics, became a radio ham operator, and went to MIT. In contrast, I grew up in a Mexican intellectual family in which language, the humanities, and the arts were of greater interest than technology, and even as a child I was exposed to conversations between my parents on parapsychology and hypnosis (my father was a psychoanalyst who championed hypnosis).

These different backgrounds partly explain why for Tart analogies to systems and circuits pervade his early thinking about ASC, whereas

I have developed more the connections of altering consciousness, arts, and the humanities (e.g., Cardeña & Winkelman, 2011). Also, I arrived at my interest in ASC via my experiences in an experimental theater group (Cardeña, 2023), whereas his interest seems to have sprung from the pages of books.

Perhaps the biggest difference, as he makes clear in a number of the interviews, was his goal to somehow resolve the conflict he sees between science and religion. In contrast, religion was never a particular concern for me despite (although I suspect "because") the fact that I went to a Catholic school, in which I observed the obtuseness and hypocrisy of most of the priests in charge of discipline. For him, a world without spirit or the possibility of survival might make life meaningless, whereas for me, values, ethics, and the quest to improve oneself and others can be justified without recourse to them (cf. Nagel, 2013).

Yet, despite these differences, we have arrived at similar destinations, including criticizing fundamentalisms of the pro- and anti-psi stripe (e.g., Cardeña, 2011), and taking a pluralist approach to the ontology and usefulness of ASC. The latter was one of the many extraordinary insights that James arrived at much earlier (James, 1902/1958). At this crossroads of our respective life roads, I hope that Charley (as he likes to be called by his friends) will not find in this foreword that: "his words come limping back from his pupil's mouth" but that "philosophy [study of consciousness in our case] is not a tool which can be passed about like a mason's rule; it is a fire struck from the glows of minds in search of truth. Without that fire, it is nothing" (Renault, 1966, pp. 49, 99),

References

Cardeña, E. (2005). The phenomenology of deep hypnosis: Quiescent and physically active. *International Journal of Clinical & Experimental Hypnosis, 53*(1), 37-59. Doi: 10.1080/00207140490914234

Cardeña, E. (2011). On wolverines and epistemological totalitarianism: Guest editorial. *Journal of Scientific Exploration, 25,* 539-551.

Cardeña, E. (2019). What the Taller de Investigación Teatral revealed to me. In N. Núñez, *Anthropocosmic theatre* (pp. 215-218). University of Huddersfield Press. https://doi.org/10.5920/anthropocosmic.09

Cardeña, E. (in press). Altered consciousness and transpersonal psychology. In G. Hartelius (Ed.), *The Wiley-Blackwell handbook of transpersonal psychology*

Cardeña, E. (2023). A festschrift for a consciousness hummingbird: Charles T. Tart [Editorial]. *Journal of Anomalous Experience and Cognition, 3*(2), 222–227. https://doi.org/10.31156/jaex.25346

Cardeña, E., Jönsson, P., Terhune, D. B., & Marcusson-Clavertz, D. (2013). The neurophenomenology of neutral hypnosis. *Cortex, 49,* 375-385. http://dx.doi.org/ 10.1016/j.cortex.2012.04.001

Cardeña, E., Lynn, S. J., & Krippner, S. (2014). *Varieties of anomalous experience.* (2ⁿᵈ Ed.). American Psychological Association.

Cardeña, E., & Marcusson-Clavertz, D. (2020). Changes in state of consciousness and psi in ganzfeld and hypnosis conditions. *Journal of Parapsychology, 84*(1). 66-84. Doi: 10.30891/jopar.2020.01.07.

Cardeña, E., & Winkelman, N. (Eds.) (2011). *Altering consciousness: Multidisciplinary perspectives.* Two volumes. Praeger.

Cunningham, P. (2023). A transpersonal festschrift to honor Charles Tart on his 85th birthday. *Journal of Anomalous Experience and Cognition, 3*(2), 228–247. https://doi.org/10.31156/jaex.24308

Ludwig, A. (1966). Altered states of consciousness. *Archives of General Psychiatry, 15*(3):225-34. doi: 10.1001/archpsyc.1966.01730150001001

Nagel. T. (2013, November 21). Ronald Dworkin: The moral quest (A review of *Ronald Dworkin,* by Stephen Guest). *The New York Review of Books. https:// www.nybooks.com/articles/2013/11/21/ronald-dworkin-moral-quest/*

Ornstein, R. (1973). *The nature of human consciousness: A book of readings.* W. H. Freeman.

Renault, M. (1966). *The mask of Apollo.* New English Library.

Tart, C. T. (1969). *Altered states of consciousness: A book of readings.* John Wiley.

Tart, C. T. (1970). Transpersonal potentialities of deep hypnosis. *Journal of Transpersonal Psychology, 2*(1), 27-40.

Tart, C. T. (1971). *On being stoned: A psychological study of marijuana intoxication.* Science and Behavior Books.

Tart, C. T. (1972). States of consciousness and state-specific sciences. *Science, 176,* 1203-1210.

Tart, C. T. (1975a). *States of consciousness.* E. P. Dutton.

Tart, C. T. (1975b). *Transpersonal psychologies: Perspectives on the mind from seven great spiritual traditions.* Harper & Row.

Tart, C. T. (1998). Six studies of out-of-body experiences. *Journal of Near-Death Studies, 7*(2), 73-99.

Introduction[3]

~

Charles T. Tart

There's no question in my mind that essential science has the potential to help us understand spirituality and perhaps make it more effective. *But* (and this is a very important but), I haven't participated in these interviews simply as a scientist.

I was raised to be religious, a Lutheran. My grandmother, who was a source of unconditional love for me, took me to Sunday school. What was good enough for her was good enough for me! I believed what they taught me in Sunday school, I tried to be good (it wasn't that easy!), and at age twelve was confirmed as a church member.

One way it wasn't easy was that when I was eight, my grandmother died unexpectedly, just dropped to the sidewalk from a heart attack.

Not long after, I came down with rheumatic fever. In those days there wasn't really any good treatment for it other than bed rest and hope. Most kids who had rheumatic fever got permanent heart damage and died of heart failure sometime in their 20s. With the wisdom of hindsight, partially gained through an enormous amount of work on spiritual growth and psychological understanding work for me, I realized that my world had come to such a tragic end with my grandmother's death, that I wanted to die—of a broken heart, no less, rheumatic fever! —and go to heaven to rejoin my grandmother.

As an adult, I can see how illogical that was, and yet I have a deep respect for my earlier self who loved that much. I was intrigued by

---

[3] This introduction is partly based on Tart (2017)

science from the time I was a child, had a chemistry and electricity laboratory in my cellar, was a Boy Scout, became a ham radio operator, etc. I've always been fascinated by ideas, but I'm also very practical. I worked my way through college, for example, as a radio engineer, keeping commercial radio station transmitters running.

As I became a teenager, I realized that adults were hypocritical in the way they practiced their religion and, even more importantly, that science conflicted with much of religion. Indeed, science seemed to think that religion was nothing but superstition and even insanity. How to reconcile that conflict with a basic faith in a God and a loving universe that was still so much a part of me?

I never claim to be an authority on the spiritual, but I am well versed in essential science. Would it help us to have a more factual, a "truer" understanding of certain phenomena that were and are important bases for religion and spirituality?

I certainly thought so by the time I was in my teens, and my career as a scientist and psychologist has focused around the themes like (a) what are real phenomena that provide some kind of a basis for religion and spirituality, (b) what kinds of things distort our understanding of religion, (c) can we have a kind of attitude toward religion that encourages the best in it and helps us, but (d) doesn't let us be carried away with superstition and prejudice, or (e) overreact to the errors in spirituality or contemporary science such that we, as the old saying puts it, throw out the baby with the bath water?

We tend to think of scientists as people who are seeking more accurate truths but believe that they shouldn't be and aren't personally engaged with their subject matter to avoid being biased. That's a noble and practical strategy in many ways. We certainly have scholars of religion who do nothing but intellectual analyses of it, often very biased analyses, and we have social scientists who look at psychological and social consequences of various religious beliefs without ever asking anything about the truth of those beliefs per se. You can be socially accepted in the social hierarchy of organized science today if you assume, explicitly or implicitly, that religious experiences are all illusions of the brain. But it's OK and useful to investigate the consequences of people believing they are real. Useful knowledge can be gained that way, although at a cost of implicitly denying any reality to spiritual matters without investigating that possible reality.

The question of whether we have souls—or, to put it more generally, whether there is any reality to the spiritual—is vitally important in a world where materialistic greed can readily support the trashing of our planet and its life, including us, the human race; and I don't think people should be effectively forbidden from accessing the scientific observations and knowledge that suggest—some would say prove, but I'm being deliberately conservative here—that there is indeed some kind of reality to "soul" and "spirit." Frozen attitudes that effectively act as a fundamentalist *Church of Materialism* tell us that spirituality is all delusion and imagination, to soothe the ignorant, while the smart ones grab the wealth and power—although then we all die anyway, and life doesn't have any meaning.

I consider science to be (or at least it can be) a noble calling, an attempt to improve our human condition by getting better knowledge of how the world (and people) function. But while the aim is noble, we who practice science, or anyone who tries to bring science to bear on practical problems, are human. We have our hopes and fears and can unthinkingly be deeply biased. Consider the story below, related to me by a trusted colleague. I have blurred some of the names and places to protect—well not quite the innocent, but perhaps innocent in being victims of their social conditioning rather than deliberately nasty—but I have had many experiences like it.

Two prominent parapsychological researchers had been invited to have a debate for an audience of several hundred writers and reporters from a major media network. The first parapsychologist, a physicist by training, presented some information about the state of our knowledge of ESP, drawing primarily on experimental results published in refereed, scientific journals. Then a prominent philosopher and "skeptic" got up and scathingly dumped all over the physicist's presentation, dismissing it all as stupid nonsense.

Then it was the turn of my colleague who told me of this incident. He pointed out to the philosopher that, ethically, one could not take such a strong and negative position on any area of knowledge without being fully conversant with the relevant literature. My colleague said that he assumed the philosopher knew the literature well and suggested that he pick any study he liked and tell him and the audience what was wrong with it. Then it could be reasonably discussed.

Without even thinking, in a voice dripping with condescension, the prominent philosopher replied, "You don't think I read this stuff, do you?"

My colleague just let that statement hang in silence. After a bit there were snickers, then chuckles, then the room filled with guffaws from the audience. The philosopher suddenly understood what he had said, and turned bright red. There was a break soon, and he didn't come back from it.

This kind of thing is why, sadly, I feel there are almost no honest, genuine "skeptics" when it comes to parapsychological and similar evidence that points to some reality to the spiritual. The Shorter Oxford English Dictionary gives a major definition of a skeptic as "A person seeking the truth; an inquirer who has not yet arrived at definite convictions." The self-styled "skeptics" I have met are, for practical purposes, true believers who already know all important truths, so they simply dismiss anything that doesn't fit their world view without bothering with actual scholarly or scientific inquiry. Since being a scientist is a high prestige role in society they claim to be scientifically trained and motivated, but they are not. The more adamant they are that the psychic and spiritual are all nonsense, the less it almost always turns out they know about the scientific evidence. Why bother to waste their time becoming informed about what they already know is nonsense? I must call them pseudo-skeptics.

As a psychologist, and as someone who has observed my own irrational defenses in action in many areas of life, I can understand this, but as a scientist it's depressing.

So, I have been personally involved in many spiritual practices throughout my life, blending these with my more scientific and intellectual attempts at understanding. Not that I'm a "believer" in any religion or spiritual path. As much as I respect the many spiritual paths and religions, I doubt that any of them have fully understood all the important truths about the universe and expressed them in ways that are eternally true. I've been misunderstood a million times in my own life when I've explained things in ways that I thought were perfectly clear and couldn't possibly be misinterpreted—but they were. Insofar as this can happen with relatively ordinary things, how much more so with things that touch on our deepest values and beliefs, or involve extraordinary ways of sensing and knowing?

So, there's been a kind of back-and-forth in my life between deep involvement in particular spiritual practices, then deep involvement in study and experimentation from the scientific and scholarly side. Sometimes the two approaches help each other, and sometimes they just make me more aware of how little I understand and what the contradictions can be. But, overall, I feel I've gotten some better understandings—at best with my heart, not only my intellect.

We have the beginning of a science of the soul but, unfortunately, what we've learned is being kept much too secret by those who believe that a total materialism is the answer to everything. By repressing this growing science, many, many people have suffered unnecessarily, as they are told by The Authorities that their profound spiritual experience is nothing but their brains acting crazy.

If you are curious about your nature, if you sincerely wonder whether there is anything more to life than that (a) we and the whole universe came about through nothing but blind chemical processes, (b) live with no inherent meaning to life other than that which helps us survive, and then (c) we die, that's the end, period, then you'll find these interviews quite interesting. If you are deeply involved in some religion or spiritual path, you may find the information presented here encouraging that you're on to something real, but I should warn: it may stimulate useful questions about some aspects of it. If your personal spiritual path teaches that you should not ask any questions—well that's not how I think knowledge progresses.

There, I've put myself in a scientifically cautious and respectable position! Except, unfortunately, I expect still to be irrationally rejected by those for whom science has hardened into a dogma, a belief system that must not be questioned, as we will, sadly, explore.

These interviews are a result of more than half a century spent looking for the soul, looking for what truth there is in religion and spirituality, based on my and colleagues' studies in parapsychology and altered states of consciousness. As I grew older, I realized that science was right about many false and crazy-making aspects of religion, and science was also quite biased and blind to ignore the fact that various religions not only gave us deep meaning, but *they also had some degree of factual support*. As a (hopefully) sophisticated adult, I now look much more sympathetically on religions as important attempts by us human beings to find meaning in life and to make sense out of the occasional deep spiritual experiences that people have. I also realized how often religion has been used as an excuse to indulge the worst of human instincts for dominance, greed, and power, so I can understand and empathize with those who are very negative about religion.

If you're wondering, dear reader, whether it's hard to research science and spirituality, then yes—there's irrational dismissal on the one hand, and imaginary "facts" on the other—but it's been a fascinating six decades of research for me! I have no regrets that I didn't stay on a safe, conventional career path and study only what was accepted by the establishment.

I'm not just a person living only in my intellect. Much of the personal growth and maturation in my life has come about by realizing that ideas, and the feelings they generate can be intoxicating to me. I'm an intellectual drunk, a "thoughtaholic." But that such ideas make me feel good doesn't make them true; all ideas should be checked, as much as possible, against reality. You can't do this for everything, of course; faith is important, but I prefer an informed faith to a blind faith.

1

Science and Spiritual Traditions

~

Recorded in 1988

Jeffrey Mishlove: Hello and welcome. Our topic today is "Science and Spiritual Traditions," and my guest, Dr. Charles Tart, is a professor of psychology at the University of California at Davis, a past president of the Parapsychological Association, and author of numerous books, including *Altered States of Consciousness, States of Consciousness, Waking Up, Transpersonal Psychologies*, and many others. Welcome, Charley.

Charles Tart: Thank you, Jeffrey.

Mishlove: It's a pleasure to have you here. More scientists are taking an interest in spiritual phenomena especially here on the West Coast, but also throughout the United States. Because of mass media and jet airplane travel, we are being exposed more to Asian spiritual traditions, and it almost seems incumbent on any thinking American to evaluate Buddhism, Hinduism, and Sufi traditions. Do we have the tools to analyze, to make sense of these traditions?

Tart: It's a good question because we traditionally think there is a conflict between science and religion because science showed that religion's claims were all false and not to be taken seriously. Yet as you say, there are a lot of scientists who are getting interested in religion, especially the Eastern spiritual disciplines. It's interesting to think about: Must these areas of science and religion conflict, or can they help each other? Could science make religion more efficient? That's a terribly Western view, of course. Could the spiritual traditions somehow add more vitality to science or make it more effective? Those are important questions that I think we can have interesting discussions about.

Mishlove: But where does one begin? There are so many stories we hear in the news about people being taken in by cults. It seems to me that our culture is very confused about what's happening here.

Tart: I don't think that's the major obstacle. Of course, there are cults, and there are people who do nasty things in the name of the spiritual. There are people like that in politics, in economics, and in every other walk of life, and I don't think that it's more prevalent in the spiritual field. We're perhaps insulted more when someone who claims to be spiritual turns out to be a con man. I think our primary problem is that we've all had some degree of scientific education. Whether you think of yourself as a scientist or not, we all must take science courses, and we are informed through the newspapers, magazines, and television. We get a worldview that seems to have left the essence of religion out. So, if you buy that scientific worldview, and we all do to some extent.

Mishlove: Godless capitalism.

Tart: Godless capitalism, or godless Marxism. If you buy the worldview, that reality is nothing but what is physical, it's only the atoms and the energies that are real, then what could spirituality be? Certainly, the aspects of it concerned with deities make no sense at all scientifically. The most they can come up with is a pseudo-liberal attitude that meditation calms people's minds in a culture that suffers from stress, so even if the religious aspect of it is nonsense, maybe it's good for your mental health. And, someday, we'll be able to give people a pill that will do the job better.

Mishlove: And we should be tolerant of other people's religions.

Tart: That attitude doesn't set you up to approach the spiritual very well. Even people I know who are very serious students of spiritual paths still go through periods of conflict, where the part of them that's been educated in science says, "What are you doing? You're hypnotizing yourself into a state of blankness, giving yourself delusions and visions that are all nonsense." Now, when we talk about a lot of scientists, especially on the West Coast, being interested, I don't think that in many cases that's because their expertise in science has led them to look at the spiritual life. Rather, I think that it's despite their expertise in science. The gaps in their life and the emptiness that comes from not having any kind of spiritual foundation have forced them to begin looking at something else.

Mishlove: There's some other part of their nature besides the scientific part that is motivated by these spiritual traditions.

Tart: Yes, I think we're inherently spiritual creatures, and I'll say that as a scientist, a psychologist, and a human being and put evidence behind it. I think parts of us are inherently spiritual, and when you deny a part of your mind and nature, that's unhealthy. It begins to create symptoms and funny behaviors until we can no longer deny it. That doesn't mean that we should believe everything that's spiritual. This is where I think science can be helpful to us. A lot of what is called "spiritual" is nonsense.

Mishlove: You mean astrology, palmistry, things of this sort?

Tart: I don't think much of astrology, but my friends who are into it say people with my sign never believe in astrology. Even the great religions have formulations of what they think spiritual life is about, that are nonsense in contemporary terms. They might have been a useful way of describing ancient realities, but the words don't mean the same thing anymore.

Mishlove: What do you mean? What's an example of that?

Tart: Take a practice like contemplation. In the Middle Ages, "contemplation" had a well-defined meaning in the religious community. Nowadays, "contemplate" to most people means to sit down and think about something. It's lost almost all its connection with certain attention-training, meditation-like practices, so the idea doesn't carry the same weight. It's also a matter of individual differences in our minds. We all are normal after a fashion, but our minds work in different ways. As a psychologist, I can come up with certain procedures that will work very well for a person with a certain type of mind, but for another type of person, it's a waste of their time. These traditional spiritual practices have been passed down for thousands of years and are so venerable, but they were designed for people brought up in different cultures with different kinds of minds. They might not work at all for most people in our culture, or they might have the opposite effect of what they were intended to have.

Mishlove: For a person who's thinking of going on a spiritual path, it's important to know something about what type of person they are, and what type of person is likely to be most benefited by particular paths.

Tart: When you put it that way, you come up against one of the great inadequacies of our knowledge. I would like to be able to say that scientists have looked at various spiritual practices as done by certain types of people and could provide a psychological test. But we don't know enough to do that. That's one of the ways that science could help the spiritual.

Mishlove: Perhaps in a few hundred years, we'll have that.

Tart: We could have reasonable approximations of it in a couple of generations if we set our mind to it. But what people must do now is try a variety of spiritual paths until they find one that works for them, where something resonates deep inside them, and something effective happens. It's trial and error at this point.

Mishlove: What about the issue of eclecticism versus following one teaching, one path? Do you have any thoughts on that?

Tart: You certainly have the extremes, don't you? On the one hand you have mystics who have said every person's path is unique. At the other end, you have people who say, "This is the way, and the steps are absolutely codified, and you mustn't deviate." For some types of people, if they can find their right path, then they should follow it very religiously. For other kinds of people to follow a path that diligently, that narrowly, will cause them to waste a lot of time and not learn from it. There's a matter of experimentation, and you must observe yourself as part of the process. Eclecticism is a way of not getting seriously involved in anything, and a lot of people use this as a defense. They may start to do some spiritual practice that begins to work, and things start opening inside. It scares the hell out of them, so they decide to go to Baba New Cuisine's lecture that night to learn about some new technique to not persist in the previous path.

Mishlove: To avoid the intensity.

Tart: Yet there are times that you have some feeling for when you should concentrate on certain kinds of spiritual practices and try to master them, but you may have plateaued on those practices or taken a dead end at other times, and you need something fresh.

Mishlove: I suppose there's a delicate line distinguishing between the real intensity of spiritual work, on the one hand, and the intensity that can come from an oppressive, dogmatic confrontation.

Tart: Yes, and I think in the long run, the only answer is self-knowledge. You must constantly concentrate on trying to know yourself more and more thoroughly, more and more deeply, so you can spot that fine line. Otherwise, you won't continue to grow; you'll settle for some kind of dogma that makes you feel good or superior.

Mishlove: Going back to the 1960s, there's been a resurgence of spiritual movements like Zen and Transcendental Meditation. Then, there was a sense in which people became concerned about what was called spiritual fascism and the danger of following a guru too obediently. Now there seems to be a new awakening with more of a balance, and a softer approach.

Tart: We had spiritual faddism along with spiritual fascism with the Guru of the Month Club. Lots of people were involved in spiritual practices mainly because they were fashionable and that's what their friends were doing, but not what they wanted. A lot of those people have dropped out. With the more serious core of people, Tibetan Buddhism and Zen Buddhism are solidly established in American culture now, although they're still not completely adapted. I see this conflict in many of the Buddhist teachers. On the one hand, there's an understandable desire to preserve the tradition because it's the way things worked for them for hundreds of years. On the other hand, you can't make Tibetans or Japanese out of Americans. You can widen them to some extent, but if you insist on preserving the spiritual practices and system wholesale, you're making it inaccessible to large numbers of Westerners.

For instance, a friend of mine spent years in Zen monasteries and eventually came back to the West. For a while, he was teaching in a very Japanese-style monastery in Los Angeles, and he realized that there were very few people he could teach Zen Buddhism to. We don't need Zen Buddhism. We need American Buddhism. In fact, we don't even need American Buddhism. We need an American practice for people to become more enlightened, more awake, more compassionate, and more effective. That's the challenge. If you have spiritual insights from some other culture, you still must adapt them. That's why I think anthropology is one of the great blessings of our time. We have precise knowledge of cultural relativity and realize how things must be translated into the culture of the people we're working with if they're going to be effective.

Mishlove: I recall a discussion I had with Idries Shah about twenty-five years ago. We were talking about what was happening in California, how excited people were, how people would smile at each other, and the way people recognized the essence of each other when they talked. Since he came from India and Afghanistan, he said, "Well, in our part of the world, this has been going on for a thousand years. We don't get so excited."

Tart: What we've done is naive in certain ways, and at the same time, it's also necessary growth. You always must take comments like this, too, from the perspective of how much is an adaptation to the culture and how much of it is holding on to the old stuff. Shah is someone I admire greatly for promoting the idea of time, place, and people, to adapt spiritual teachings to a culture. And yet, at the same time, if you say, "We've been doing this for thousands of years and not excited by it," that takes some of the vitality out of what people are doing. I feel delicate about that kind of remark.

Mishlove: For scientists who want to maintain the value of the scientific method, how far do you think it is appropriate or reasonable to expect them to go into the spiritual realm? How far is it integrable?

Tart: I think we can go further than we think we can. In my experience, the traditional conflict between science and religion has been between third-rate religionists and third-rate scientists. It's been between scientists who are insecure in their own discipline and not that bright about it, so they need to defend it, or between religionists who are insecure and mustn't ask any questions about their religions. The first-rate scientist knows not only the good side of science but also knows the limitations with humility and excitement about what can be done.

The same thing applies to a first-class spiritual practitioner. He or she knows that they are working within a system, a human formulation, and it's got its limits. If both people are committed to truth and have a sense of humility, then how can there be conflict? There's a saying that's attributed to the mythical Sarmoung brotherhood regarding religious ideas: "There's no God but reality. To seek him elsewhere is the action of the fall." As a psychologist, I've always found that statement to be profound, because the interpretation I take of it is that the idea of God, which includes the idea of everything, has to include everything that is. As soon as you say, "No, God is good, and God is A, B, and C, but not E, F, and G," psychologically, you have partial perception, tuning out some things and overemphasizing others. We know what happens when you have partial perception: You get an unbalanced view of the world, you make stupid decisions based on that false information, and you create suffering.

I don't think that anyone who seeks the truth about spiritual paths can quarrel with the idea that there is no God but reality. No scientist could quarrel with that if he's interested in the search for truth. There may be some conflicts at some very high level, but most of it is unnecessary. The conflict I worry about is that religion has often been presented as a path of faith: you're to believe certain things and base your whole life and practices around them. Whereas science is traditionally presented as a path of doubt. According to science, the explanation that doesn't get knocked down after we try hard to do so is provisionally the best one. That doesn't square with a simple faith, and they're both very powerful. Obviously, science has gone a long way practicing this path of doubt. Obviously, some spiritual people have gone a long way practicing faith. Faith is tricky because you can get caught up in blind, ignorant faith, where you can put all your energies into something that turns out to be false. Doubt can also become very corrosive, so that the quality of people's lives can be just eroded away till they're empty.

Mishlove: There's also something akin to blind, ignorant doubt, I think, as well.

Tart: Yes, you can come up with all these interesting categories. What I'm struggling with, and I'm still not quite clear on, is how to reconcile a path of doubt and a path of faith. How do you balance those, so you get the best of both, without the corrosive or the blinding effects?

Mishlove: Charley, you're one of the foremost parapsychologists. You've done dozens of research studies in parapsychology, and surely this must be one science, if there's any science, that bridges these two worlds.

Tart: That to me is the main importance of parapsychology that stuff like telepathy, clairvoyance, and precognition is going on, and they don't fall into any kind of reasonable physical explanation. It tells you to keep your mind open to the possibility of spiritual realities that I think is its main function for our times and it's scientific. Parapsychologists are using science in a very hard-nosed, rigorous kind of way. We set up experiments according to our physical view of the world so that nothing unusual should happen. Nevertheless, the subject picks up some of the thoughts from another person who is isolated in another room miles away. If it shouldn't happen in terms of what I know about the physical world, but it is happening, that tells me that my view of the physical world isn't complete.

Parapsychology is a long way from proving the reality of specific spiritual concepts, which is going to take a lot more research. But it does say that we know that the mind is not necessarily limited to the inside of your head. It can reach out. The mind is not necessarily limited to the present time. It seems to reach into the future. Just "simple" things like that tell you it's a big and interesting universe. So, if somebody talks about their praying having an effect, I'm not going to *a priori* say that can't be because maybe it involves telepathy.

Mishlove: Many of the skeptics criticize parapsychologists for encouraging credulity and gullibility in the populace. I think there may be an issue there. How does one maintain the balance of being open-minded to the possibility of psychic phenomena, and yet not swallow so many stories hook, line, and sinker?

Tart: There's a real issue and a pseudo-issue there. I think parapsychologists have an almost zero net effect on increasing anybody's credulity. People have such an enormous amount of credulity to begin with that the experimental data of parapsychology is a drop in the bucket. Credulity is a problem because there are people who will believe anything if it's labeled spiritual or psychical, and I think they make a lot of mistakes by believing nonsense. I have a hard time getting across to people the idea of balance in this area. Yes, you should be open-minded, but your mind should not have holes in it where everything just goes through. There is still a need for evaluation and understanding.

Parapsychology, as an experimental science, opens our limits and says some of the spiritual things may be real according to scientific criteria. That's a long way from learning any wisdom, emotional balance, or spiritual development. Parapsychology is a basic science for learning things about the spiritual, but it's not an applied science for the art of living.

Mishlove: Is there anything from your experience in parapsychology that would be useful to provide guidelines for people who encounter psychic experiences, or claims of psychic experience, within spiritual traditions?

Tart: Yes. For instance, all spiritual traditions have the same set of paranormal phenomena. Every miracle that tradition A claims, traditions B and C will also claim. Each one interprets it in a narrow-minded way to prove they're right and everybody else is wrong. Almost any spiritual tradition will have occasionally produced psychic phenomena that have been interpreted as miracles that seem to validate the tradition.

Mishlove: No one has a monopoly on that.

Tart: Right. You must look beyond that. In terms of personal development, you have to ask what are these being used for and what do they contribute? Someone may have miraculously figured out what was on my mind, but what was the quality of the advice they gave me for growth? Just because you can get information doesn't mean you offer good advice.

Mishlove: In other words, to not be so swayed by psychic evidence that we automatically link that with spiritual authority.

Tart: Spiritual authority has to be evaluated on its own basis, not because it can pull off something psychic once in a while. I've known a lot of psychics and some of them have struck me as very spiritual people. They have depth, compassion, openness, and maturity that's wonderful. Other psychics I know, who are just as psychic, are real neurotics and I wouldn't ask their advice on how to live because they're no more integrated or mature than the rest of us. You can make a bad mistake if you mistakenly interpret it as spiritual ability.

Mishlove: I think there's one area that many people are uncertain about, because at times when people need healing, they are desperate, and they may turn to spiritual traditions. Are there any guidelines you can offer?

Tart: I think because someone may heal you in an unconventional fashion or use an apparent psychic skill, doesn't necessarily make them a spiritual authority. My doctor heals me in all sorts of ways that are quite mysterious to me at times but that doesn't mean my doctor is a spiritual person. On a deeper level, I think there is an intrinsic connection between an overall healing and a spiritual attitude toward life, but that's not the same as being able to cure very specific problems. I don't feel like there's a very satisfactory answer because it's not clear in my mind.

Mishlove: There's the paradox. On the one hand parapsychologists may come up with a scientific explanation for psychic phenomena which would almost totally remove them from the realm of the spiritual. On the other hand, at least to some degree, there are instances in which spiritual traditions may have some deep knowledge of psychic phenomena, and there's a link there.

Tart: There's an implicit assumption behind what you say, that to be spiritual something must be mysterious. I want to raise some interesting questions about that assumption. A lot of the great mystics have said we're surrounded by miracles all day long, but because we're used to them, we pay no attention to them. Ordinary life is an incredible spiritual experience if you open your mind and wake up to it. But if you don't pay attention, it's just that familiar stuff all the time and you don't get the message.

Mishlove: That must be the ultimate lesson of the spiritual path, I suppose.

Tart: A lot of people make the connection that the spiritual is mysterious. I don't think that's a very solid basis to have a good spiritual life on.

Mishlove: In other words, auras, healing, telepathy, past lives, and spirit guides may ultimately have very little to do with a genuine spiritual life.

Tart: I think the real test of people's spirituality comes out in simple ways. Are they decent to a clerk who doesn't wait on them properly? Are they too superior to deal with people who have bad karma? There is a whole side to the spiritual life that involves unusual experiences and mystical insights, but if spirituality doesn't manifest as compassion, decency, and intelligence in ordinary life, I think it's very shallow.

Mishlove: That seems to be a guideline that applies to Asian traditions ultimately.

Tart: Yes. An excellent example of science contributing to the spiritual path is the use of psychology to see how we use things for ulterior motives. Psychologists can be of immense help to see if your spirituality is genuine or if it is a mask for feelings of negative self-worth that you don't want to deal with.

Mishlove: Charley, I think we've got the point that psychology can help us see if we may have other motives that are influencing our spiritual search.

Tart: Psychology is part of reality, too.

Mishlove: Charley Tart, thank you very much for being with me.

Tart: Thank you, Jeffrey.

2

Self-Observation

~

Recorded in 1988

Jeffrey Mishlove: Our topic today is "Self-Observation," and my guest is Professor Charles Tart, a member of the Department of Psychology at the University of California at Davis, a past president of the Parapsychological Association, and the author of numerous books, including *Transpersonal Psychologies, States of Consciousness, Altered States of Consciousness*, and most recently, *Waking Up*. Welcome, Charley.

Charles Tart: I'm glad to be here, Jeff.

Mishlove: It's a pleasure to have you here. When we talk about self-observation, I think a lot of people feel a little embarrassed. It's as though if they begin to observe themselves, they get self-conscious, and they blush a little bit. It's almost as if there's a subconscious agreement among people not to look too closely at themselves.

Tart: Yes, that's one of the sad parts about this whole field. So many of us have been taught or conditioned in childhood that we're not good enough or lacking, and that makes us very reluctant to look at ourselves. If we don't learn how to find out what we're like, then we don't use our minds efficiently and make all sorts of mistakes. So, we have to learn to self-observe, but it has to be done very carefully.

Anthropologists have determined several ways of controlling people. One way is to have guards follow them around, which is an expensive method. Those guards aren't doing anything else productive because they're watching you all the time. A much more efficient way is to put a guard in a child's head and split their mind so that a part of their mind absorbs all the standards that the parents and society want them to have and watch for transgressions. Freud talked about it as the superego, this part of us that's over our ordinary conscious self and can make us feel bad. I want to talk about the value of self-observation, but I'm not talking about superego observation because most of us already know how to do that, and we feel bad, right? We selectively watch ourselves and catch ourselves in a fault, sin, or lack, and then we feel rotten about it.

Mishlove: When other people want us to look at ourselves, it's to make us feel guilty about something we've done.

Tart: Exactly. We lay a lot of guilt trips on each other to try to control each other. So, it's not surprising that most people don't want to look inside. Instead, they distract themselves.

Mishlove: It's as if self-observation becomes associated with feelings of guilt.

Tart: Exactly. Most people can think of times from their childhood when they were in a difficult situation and were trying to get out of it, and one or the other parent said, "Be honest. Look at yourself. Tell me the truth." That whole idea of knowing the truth about yourself, or revealing that truth to others, became associated with fear, punishment, and feeling rotten.

Mishlove: In a religious sense, it even gets associated with sin. It's not just your parents; it's like God is judging.

Tart: Exactly. That's what makes the superego so powerful. There's another distinction you can make. Anthropologists say that in some cultures, shame controls people: if someone knew what you did, you would be so ashamed. However, it has a little "out." You can be tempted to get away with it if nobody knows it is you. The superego is one step better because even if nobody else knows, *you* know, and *God* knows, and so you get punished for even thinking about doing things.

Mishlove: Are you suggesting that people in some of these primitive cultures don't have superegos but that they are unique to our culture?

Tart: It's certainly not unique to our culture, but there are some cultures in which the superego is a very minor part of a given person's mind. Our culture today is mixed. We've drifted more toward a shaming culture when transgressions become public. But we were once primarily a superego culture. That comes from our whole Judeo-Christian heritage. God is watching.

Mishlove: So, guilt and the fear of punishment, is one of the forces that mitigates self-observation.

Tart: Right.

Mishlove: Are there some other major obstacles to self-observation?

Tart: Oh, sure. We're not taught self-observation. The whole culture tells us that we're not good, so we don't want to look. The Freudian notion is that, basically, we're wild animals with a thin veneer of civilization on top that is keeping us from running amok. Who wants to look inside at this picture?

Mishlove: Sex and aggression.

Tart: Right. Or if you're born to original sin and basically, you're rotten and going to hell, who wants to look at that? Our culture has invented a multitude of ways to distract ourselves from ever having to look inside. But the result is that although we try to avoid the pain of seeing what we fear we'll see, then we'll mess up our lives because we don't know ourselves. We don't know what we're like, what we want, our resourcefulness, and we make mistakes.

Mishlove: And yet we have this ancient philosophical tradition, which I think goes back at least to Socrates, who said, "Man, know thyself." But when I studied philosophy in college, there was none of that.

Tart: You didn't have Introspection 101 and 102?

Mishlove: None, no. Introspection is outlawed even in psychology pretty much these days.

Tart: Not only is it effectively banned, but we don't have the skill to introspect very well. It's one thing to tell somebody, "Start observing yourself. See how you feel, what's going on." But if people take that seriously, they often find that it's very hard to concentrate, and their attention drifts. They get confused as to what they're looking at, and soon, they end up watching TV or distracting themselves again.

Mishlove: What you're saying reminds me of when I was an undergraduate psychology student back at the University of Wisconsin in the 1960s. I helped form the Psychology Students' Association, and I was elected to be the vice president. I gave a little speech saying, "I became a psychology major in order to know myself, and I'm not learning that in this department."

Tart: I bet your fellow students loved it, but it didn't go over well with the faculty.

Mishlove: I got a standing ovation at the time, but I doubt much has changed in academic psychology since then, either.

Tart: Not much. There has been a little loosening up. Even behaviorists now talk about verbal reports of fantasy behavior. But still, no recognition that we need to systematically observe our own minds.

Mishlove: This should be the goal of psychology, I think.

Tart: I wouldn't want to make it as *the* goal because we have learned a lot by concentrating on observing people externally. One of the things that you learn when you practice self-observation is that you fool yourself because you're a very biased observer. It can be helpful to get feedback from somebody else. Take a classic case in therapy. When somebody goes into therapy, and the therapist asks, "Do you get along with your father?" And the client says, "Yeah, I get along just fine." The therapist says, "Really? No problems at all?" "No!" The client says. The client isn't observing himself very well. In fact, we now know there are systematic psychological blocks involved. But the therapist can see there is a big discrepancy between the behavior and the report, and that suggests that he might learn a lot from introspection. So, we need both feedback from other people and how they perceive us, as well as self-observation.

Mishlove: Is this art of self-observation the goal of any discipline at all?

Tart: No. Many spiritual disciplines put very little emphasis on self-observation because they believe they know what's right, and they simply give you a prescription: you behave according to this set of rules, and you'll have salvation. Many spiritual disciplines may practice a very biased type of self-observation that involves the superego: here are the sins you must watch out for. So, you become very sensitive to sin. The kind of self-observation I'm talking about involves making a commitment to learn the truth about yourself and your world, no matter what it is. It's not to catch yourself in your sins, when you happen to be doing something you like or support what you already believe, but to observe yourself in your world to see what's *there*. That's a commitment.

I like to quote a famous American leader, Patrick Henry: "Eternal vigilance is the price of freedom." If you aren't vigilant about yourself, with a commitment to knowing reality as it is, you'll live in this state that I call "consensus trance". You become lost in fantasies that are widely shared within the culture because everybody else has similar fantasies. We all think we're normal, but we're cut off from the world around us and do a lot of stupid things as a result.

Mishlove: Yet it seems to me that there is a paradox there because not only is the world as it is, but it is as we create it. We're not just passive in this process.

Tart: That's right. One of the things you learn from observing yourself is that you aren't just absorbing information. Currently, you're being selective by listening to only part of the conversation. But that's fine. What you're seeking to learn through self-observation is how to run your psychological machinery, and when you do, you say, "OK, can I see more clearly? Can I see what's behind that? What else can I learn about this?" It must be done with a commitment to accept whatever you learn. It can't be to have an insight that shows how wonderful you are or what an awful sinner you are. It must be what's the truth in yourself. The truth is very rewarding in a subtle kind of way, even if you don't like what you see. I don't know how many times, in practicing self-observation, I've seen things in myself that I don't like at all, that I'm ashamed of. And yet, there's an authenticity that comes from trying to be as honest as you can.

Mishlove: This might be something like the Hegelian dialectic. You come to one point of view about yourself, and then you might notice that the opposite point of view is also true sometimes. Then, you begin to develop a synthesis and then discover something in opposition to that synthesis, and so on.

Tart: Sometimes, before that synthesis occurs, you must live with the opposition for a long period of time. I'll give you an example of self-observation, which I began doing systematically many years ago. I noticed my mental attitude when I was driving, and I realized that I was very angry at drivers who did not follow the rules. If they followed too closely behind me or cut in too closely in front of me, I didn't like that.

In fact, as I observed it more, I realized I was so angry that I wanted them to die. Anybody who followed me too closely and threatened my life deserved to die. I didn't like that about myself because I think that I am a kind, understanding person. I was going to watch it a few more times until it went away, but it didn't go away for three years. Every time I got in the car, part of me wanted to kill whenever anybody followed too close. It didn't matter that I didn't like it. I had to stay with it. Eventually, keeping the focus of consciousness there made some changes occur.

Mishlove: What you're saying is that simple observation of yourself doesn't cause change.

Tart: Sometimes, observation alone will allow for change. There are a lot of things that, in a psychological sense, aren't very potent and not hooked in with real deep, powerful emotions. These are habits of thought, feeling, and perception, and they run in the subconscious. Once the light of awareness is put on them two or three times, they just fade away.

Mishlove: You can chase away the little imps, but not the big demons.

Tart: Right. Some of those issues won't go away, and you must commit yourself to observing them even more closely and observing the emotions associated with them. Eventually, you may gain some insights to make them go away, or you may have to get some kind of training or discipline.

Mishlove: Now, when you drive your car, you don't get angry at other drivers anymore, is that right?

Tart: It's not anywhere near as bad now and I don't pay as much attention to it. Now, I get mad at the people who don't signal their left-hand turns until they're making the turn and not allowing me time to move over into the other lane. When I first started self-observation, I thought I should be able to do this for a month and become a perfect being. It's a long haul, but it's satisfying.

Mishlove: Are there particular techniques that you would recommend for people?

Tart: Yes. It's no good just to tell somebody that they should observe themselves. That's like saying, "Be good." You have to practice. You must start with learning to focus your attention clearly. If most people try a concentration exercise, like looking at the sweep-second hand or digital display on their watch, and not think of anything else, most people will find that they're lucky if ten seconds can go by before they're wondering when it will be over and what's for lunch tomorrow. You know, the mind wanders.

Mishlove: It's very hard to lock in on just one item.

Tart: Yes. And as you begin to observe yourself, you find that's one of the main qualities of ordinary consciousness. We're constantly distracted and drift to something else. We can't concentrate in a very real sense.

Mishlove: We've got so many billions of neurons that want to keep busy, I suppose.

Tart: They want to keep busy, but they're not in control. Once you see that this is difficult, you can begin practicing in simple ways. For instance, as we sit here right now, are you aware of your position in the chair? What do your arms feel like as you sit there in that chair? Are you breathing fully? Can you notice your breathing and still be aware of what I'm talking about at this moment? When you shook your head just then, how much was that a conscious decision, and how much was it habitual? You can't expect to start self-observation and see these fantastic things about yourself right away because that's a biased observation. You have to say, "For the next five minutes, I'm going to see every little thing that comes along, even if it's trivial, even if I don't think it's important," because that trains you to pay attention, and that's the foundation.

Mishlove: In other words, you would recommend people isolating a small block of time, like five minutes, to pay attention, and notice everything.

Tart: Sure. If I tell somebody to observe themselves for the next hour, they will observe themselves for only two or three minutes if they're lucky and then forget about it. Then when they remember it again, they feel guilty because they had forgotten. You set yourself up for failure to do it for an hour right off. Start at 30 seconds or when you get good, five minutes. Notice when you walk down the street, how you move your arms, or when you sit in a room with nothing to do, what you look at. Is there a pattern in the way you look around the room? Start with simple, non-threatening things. Don't start right away by observing being nasty to people. That's heavy and will cause a lot of resistance.

If you learn to focus on the simple things, then you can get into the more complex things that are emotionally relevant.

Mishlove: Do you recommend, then, that people keep a journal, or notes of these observations?

Tart: I am ambivalent about that. If you self-observe to get interesting material to write in your journal, you're going to be selective. Who's going to write in their journal about an itch in their left elbow that spread down to their left wrist? Nobody's going to write that in a journal because people want a dramatic and important journal. That's selective attention. There's nothing wrong with selective attention at certain times, especially if you do it voluntarily.

Mishlove: But you're suggesting it's important to notice the seemingly trivial things.

Tart: Yes, to stay in the here and now. Self-observation ultimately leads to an ability to be present to what's going on. Let's face it: sometimes, in the present, nothing spectacular is happening. While you're sitting here, your elbow is itching.

Mishlove: You're also suggesting, then, that physiological self-awareness is important, and by self, you mean the body.

Tart: Our bodies are full of sensations that form excellent reference points to start self-observation, but I'm not limiting it to that, of course. If something emotional happens, it's very useful to observe your emotions as if you were a fair and neutral observer. Suppose you are a reporter having to write up an objective account of what this person is feeling, but at the same time, those feelings are happening in you, so you're not completely distinct. You try to see what you feel instead of what you would like to feel or what you ought to feel. And then you gain insights into yourself.

Mishlove: The last thing a person should start to look at is the melodrama that we're all involved in.

Tart: A person can certainly start there, but it may be hard, and the superego may pick it up. Now that's another important part of self-observation. If you already have a harsh superego—and a lot of people do—and you systematically pay more attention to yourself, you're going to see a lot of things you don't like. Your superego's going to say, "Ha! Gotcha! Look at your nasty thoughts about that person." You then have to uplevel a little bit and observe the superego in action instead of just identifying with it or being carried away with it. It's an important distinction to make and an important warning. Don't underestimate the power of the superego.

Whenever you see someone who's suicided, you see the power of the superego in action: "You are so bad that you deserve only death." Another of my favorite examples: there have been a few cases in England where a house has caught on fire, and the firemen knew the person was right inside the front door and could have gotten out. They saw movement through the curtains, but the person died from smoke inhalation or being burned. It turned out they were naked, and they couldn't go out the door when they were naked.

Mishlove: They would have been mortified.

Tart: Yes, the superego made them feel ashamed enough of being naked that it amounted to a choice to die instead. The superego is very powerful, far too powerful in many cases.

Mishlove: That's remarkable. In self-observation, then, we want to observe our superego to understand its power over us.

Tart: Yes, but don't start with the superego. Start with simple things: how do you feel right now? You mentioned I focused a lot on the body. A lot of our emotions express themselves through bodily feelings. When you think you're looking at your physical sensations, you're learning to tune in to the subtleties of your emotions.

Mishlove: In other words, an itch might not be just an itch, it might be reflecting some kind of deeper level of experience.

Tart: That's right. What does the itch turn into? What's the feeling tone that goes with the itch?

Mishlove: If the itch could talk, what would it say?

Tart: Right, and you can have somebody ask you things like that, as in gestalt therapy. Certain kinds of therapy, like gestalt, can be very useful when an outsider takes up the function of a neutral observer. That's fine for certain special occasions, but you can't have a gestalt therapist or someone following you around all day and night. You must learn to be your own observer, to understand yourself better.

Mishlove: As we observe ourselves, and then observe ourselves observing ourselves, gradually, slowly, layer by layer, we become enlarged as human beings.

Tart: Yes, we get a much wider idea of who we are. When we get conditioned into a consensus trance, our human potential becomes narrowed. We could be so many things, but society decides what is good and bad, and our self-concept is narrowed, squeezed, and tightened, and we become very sad after a while. G.I. Gurdjieff expressed it very powerfully when he said a lot of people you see walking around in the street are dead. Their inner psychological selves have been so squeezed that their behavior is habit and conditioning, and their essence and vitality are all gone. It's sad.

Mishlove: It reminds me of another well-known phrase by Socrates, that the unexamined life is not a life worth living.

Tart: When we don't observe ourselves, we condemn ourselves to an unexamined life. There's another important obstacle to self-observation. Sometimes, people will perform a limited self-observation because they know something is wrong. Their life isn't going right, or there are obvious problems, or it's empty. So, they observe themselves for a while, and they see part of what's wrong, but because they want to change so badly, they see only one or two ways that they're not living right. They may convert to some religion that claims to save them from that particular thing or concentrate on some particular growth thing, without getting a good idea of what the rest of their mind is like.

Mishlove: Without continuing the process.

Tart: Yes, they stop the process.

Mishlove: I would imagine there's a lot of social pressure. Alan Watts wrote the book about the conspiracy …

Tart: *The Taboo Against Knowing Who You Are.*

Mishlove: Yes. If other people around me start to observe themselves and know themselves well, then it begins to put some pressure on me.

Tart: We talked earlier about how people try to make each other feel guilty to manipulate each other. Sometimes we try to make others have insights, but we want you to have the insights we approve of. There was a time when consciousness-raising groups were very popular. But as near as I could tell, consciousness-raising meant that when you agreed with the correct views, your consciousness was raised. You should start self-observation, not with the idea that there are certain truths that somebody else has already figured out for themselves, but with a much more open-ended idea that you want to know for yourself: I want to see things the way they are.

Mishlove: Regardless of the outcome.

Tart: I've mentioned the negative sides of self-observation, and I don't want to leave the impression that all you ever see are these horrible sides of yourself. A lot of the sides of ourselves that have been repressed are very positive, such as our vitality, our childlike joy at being alive, and a lot of our creativity and talents.

Mishlove: And certainly, our spirituality.

Tart: Yes, our spirituality is in there, too, underneath our education.

Mishlove: As a parapsychologist, you would agree that we probably would begin observing psychic phenomena or experiences.

Tart: Yes, I think psychic powers could easily emerge as a natural result of expanding your concept of who you are through self-observation.

Mishlove: Do you have a sense of where this all ends, I mean, without trying to preprogram? Because everyone needs to discover it themselves.

Tart: No, I have no sense of where it ends, and I don't want to have a sense of where it ends. It's easy to fall into this trap of reaching some final point, like being dead or something. I think it's much more exciting and adventurous to just realize there's more. It's an infinite universe so why set limits on yourself? As a psychologist, I know that if you set limits on yourself, those limits will become true most of the time.

Mishlove: Charley, this has been a very interesting discussion. We've moved from the fear and guilt associated with self-observation to the powerful aspects, the creativity, and the enlarged sense of being. It's been a pleasure having that discussion with you and seeing the range of possibilities, as well as some very practical techniques for self-exploration.

Tart: Observing myself as I talk about this, I see that I feel like an excited kid.

Mishlove: Charley Tart, thank you very much for being with me.

Tart: Thanks for creating the opportunity.

Mishlove: My pleasure.

3

Understanding ESP

~

Recorded in 1994

Jeffrey Mishlove: Our topic tonight is developing extrasensory perception. My guest, Dr. Charles Tart, is a psychologist and parapsychologist who has written *Learning to Use Extrasensory Perception* and several other books in parapsychology, including *Psi: Studies in the Scientific Realm*.

Welcome, Charley.

Charles Tart: Good evening, Jeffrey.

Mishlove: It's a pleasure to have you here. Many years ago, you pioneered ESP studies using a computerized model that provided people with instantaneous feedback. I think that's a good starting point for discussing developing psychic abilities.

Tart: Yes, it was very interesting because I never planned it. It all started with a course on human learning in graduate school that I was required to take but didn't want to because I thought it was a very dull subject. Then, years later, I started looking at parapsychological lab research where people are tested for their ESP, particularly the old classical methods such as guessing the order of a deck of cards. After they're done, somebody scores the hit rate. I started thinking about that from the learning point of view and how something is learned. You try something—you don't know what to do yet—but you try something, and you get some feedback. Was I right or wrong? If I was wrong, I know that's not the way to do it. If I were right, I'd like to repeat that behavior.

I realized that people were usually tested for psychic abilities and didn't get any feedback about being right or wrong until long after they'd tried it, which is too late for learning. In conventional psychological terms, that's how you kill off an ability and how you confuse someone, so they lose their talent.

Mishlove: It's called an extinction model.

Tart: Right. It's extinguishing behavior. So, I had an insight that if you want to effectively learn to use ESP, after your responses trying to use ESP, there needs to be immediate feedback so you can figure out what works. That's how it all got started.

Mishlove: Conversely, one of the difficulties that parapsychologists have had in getting their work accepted is that once they get a good scoring subject, they train that subject not to do well.

Tart: If you looked at the records of experiments, you would see that even the very best subjects eventually lost their abilities when they repeatedly went through card guessing.

Mishlove: So, you basically decided to use the feedback model to see if people would increase their scores rather than decline.

Tart: Right.

Mishlove: And you met with quite a bit of success.

Tart: Yes, I'm very pleased with the research to date. It also frustrates me because parapsychology is a very small field. There's not much research going on. So, with what I and some others have been able to do, the outcome of this research is that if you give immediate feedback, you will eliminate this decline. People do not get worse when they get immediate feedback. They at least hold on to what they can do. A few of them seem to improve, but there hasn't been enough research to see if some people will get good and stable using this kind of learning. So that's why I'm frustrated. This may be the key to teaching reliable ESP performance. Or, like any scientific theory, it could be a plausible-sounding idea that doesn't quite work.

Mishlove: You've explored a few other avenues for facilitating ESP besides feedback, haven't you?

Tart: Oh yes, many conditions affect how a person can use their ESP, and there must be some way to make them all work in your favor. For example, many studies have found it helps when a person is relaxed but not too relaxed. If they're too relaxed, they go to sleep.

Mishlove: Taking Valium does not increase ESP scores. What else would facilitate ESP?

Tart: A procedure known as the Ganzfeld procedure helps ESP in some people. To put it in a fancy way, your eyes are covered with translucent acetate hemispheres.

Mishlove: Ping-pong balls.

Tart: Right, ping-pong balls, exactly. It's low-budget research. But you put these ping-pong balls on so you see a completely uniform white field with a light shining on them. This makes it very easy for images to come to mind. Pretty soon, you start seeing all sorts of things. This has helped a lot of people bring up images using ESP ability which is often related to what someone in another room is trying to send.

Mishlove: Then there would be other environmental conditions that might affect ESP scoring.

Tart: Yes, the one I've been working with most, lately, is very curious. It involves some work by a man named Andrija Puharich, who did some research on this many years ago, but the scientific community largely ignored it.

Mishlove: The notorious Andrija Puharich, who discovered Uri Geller, wrote a book on psychedelic mushrooms and did a few other disreputable things.

Tart: He did some very interesting research, and I could never quite decide whether it was solid or not, so I wanted to repeat it. I eventually used a very special environment known as a Faraday cage. The great physicist Michael Faraday found that a hollow metal container prevented electrical effects from the outside from penetrating the inside. It's the principle used today to make shielded rooms of all sorts.

Puharich had found that if you put people in one of these Faraday cages— it was made from solid copper and was airtight — and it's connected to the earth using a big wire running to a rod that goes into the ground, that seemed to improve their ESP scores. But if he broke that electrical connection to the earth, so it's electrically floating, their ESP scores got worse than they would under ordinary conditions.

I thought that was strange because, given what we know about the physics of Faraday cages, that finding doesn't make sense. On the other hand, ESP doesn't make any sense regarding physics, so that didn't bother me too much. I decided to see whether this was true and designed it so people wouldn't know what was expected to happen and not be influenced psychologically.

In 1984, my students and I ran a very well-controlled double-blind study in which nobody knew exactly what was happening except me, and I stayed out of the picture. We had people do a telepathy test either with the cage grounded to the earth or electrically floating. Sure enough, people showed significant evidence of ESP when that cage was grounded, just as Puharich had found, but not when it was electrically floating.

Mishlove: Could you describe a telepathy test for the benefit of some readers who might not know what one is?

Tart: For the version I used, the receiver in the Faraday cage held a three-foot-diameter circular board on his lap with ten cards placed in slots around it. A sender in another room had a similar board with ten matching cards. At the start of the experiment, the sender randomized the cards on his or her board, and then the receiver had fifteen minutes to completely cut off from sensory contact to try to arrange his to come out the same way.

Mishlove: It's like they're both playing solitaire.

Tart: Yes, but it's a tough test. You'll generally get zero or maybe one match each time and getting as many as three is quite rare. You're getting into hundred-to-one odds against that happening by chance. Nevertheless, we got results. I'm excited about that because, again, it doesn't quite make sense regarding the physics.

Mishlove: But it happened while the cage was grounded to the earth, not otherwise. What does it imply to you?

Tart: It implies to me that we may have either a practical amplifier of telepathic ability or a shield from telepathic ability. I hesitate to say the latter because I get too many phone calls from people who think the CIA is beaming telepathic messages at them, and I don't want them putting their heads in metal.

Mishlove: All they have to do is hide in a Faraday cage, and they'll be safe.

Tart: The big problem in ESP laboratory research is that ESP is unreliable. It tends to come and go, and we don't know why, or if it's there, it's weak. So, anything that increases the strength and reliability of ESP is a very valuable step forward for research.

Mishlove: Did the positive scores you achieved in this study exceed the kinds of positive scores you would normally get in other studies that you do?

Tart: No. But then I generally do studies that work out very well.

Mishlove: You have quite a track record of successful ESP studies. One might argue, Charley, that you somehow influence the study, not the Faraday cage.

Tart: I've been accused of that, that I'm just a psychic experimenter unknowingly manipulating things in my own consciousness.

Mishlove: You're a shaman pretending to be a professor of psychology.

Tart: Perhaps it's true. That's why I made sure that I did not know exactly when the tests were going on, much less what the electrical condition was. I am not interested in discovering that I can make the world look like what I already believe it to be. That's not terribly exciting.

Mishlove: But you're testing ESP, Charley. How can you make sure you don't know? I mean, if you assume ESP works ...?

Tart: I would have had to psychically monitor when the experiments went on, figure out psychically what the conditions were, and psychically push things around to make them happen. Not only that, I would have had to look into my future a year in advance to discover something I was going to get quite interested in but had no interest in at any time and then influence my results to correlate with something that happens to the whole planet.

Mishlove: That sounds just like the sort of thing shamans like you normally do. I don't have any problem with that.

Tart: It's too grandiose for me. But let me tell you about this other result which is very interesting. During the Parapsychological Association meetings in 1985, a couple of researchers (Michael Persinger at Laurentian University and Marcia Adams at the Time Research Institute in Woodside) reported that they had compared laboratory ESP performance with the earth's geomagnetic field. Most people would say, "the geomagnetic field, what's that?" We know compasses point north. But it turns out that compasses point north, and the strength and angle of the earth's magnetic field vary slightly. Sunspots affect them; weather affects them, the rotation of the planet does, and the moon does. There are a lot of little changes there, so we have planetary magnetic weather, as it were. There are some days when the planetary magnetic field is kind of low and steady all day long and other days when it jiggles around a lot, gets strong and weak, and has a lot of changes; they're referred to as stormy days.

Adams found from some laboratory research at SRI International in remote viewing that remote viewing tended to work much better when the geomagnetic field had been quiet the day before.

Mishlove: The day before?

Tart: The day before the experiment. Persinger, on the other hand, looked at spontaneous psychic experiences, the kind people have at home. He looked at several different case collections and found that in every one of them, the geomagnetic field tended to be much lower on days of spontaneous psychic experiences. Particularly, these were psychic experiences of the telepathic type where you suddenly knew what was going on with a loved one at a distance. It didn't work with precognition. But Persinger found this thing on the day of the event, so I thought that was interesting. Remember, all this happened a year after I did my Faraday cage experiment.

Mishlove: Did they have strong correlations?

Tart: Yes, these were not little bitty effects, but they were big enough to be interesting. The promise of their work was that this effect would be strong enough that if you were getting ready to do an ESP experiment, you would call up your local magnetic weather station as it were, and if they said, "It's stormy today." You'd say, "Sorry folks, let's go home and try it another day. It's probably not going to work well today."

Mishlove: You mean to check for sunspots and things of that type.

Tart: Right. If this worked out, you could improve ESP by working on calm magnetic days instead of stormy ones.

Mishlove: I suppose it implies that our nervous system is somehow affected or the carrier wave, whatever that might be, is affected.

Tart: This is a controversial area. People are just beginning to do good research on the geomagnetic field and its effects on all sorts of behavior, but it looks as if these magnetic fields may somehow affect your nervous system. Maybe on a stormy magnetic day, it jiggles your nervous system and makes it noisy.

Mishlove: Astrologers have long made claims like this. They say that the positions of the planets affect the Earth's magnetic field.

Tart: I think there's almost no effect due to the position of the planets, so let's not go off into astrology. My astrological friends all tell me that people born under my sign never believe in astrology anyway, so what can I say? Wouldn't it be interesting if the planetary magnetic field affected the results of my Faraday cage experiment? I looked back at the data, and sure enough, they were. If I were being a shaman and just doing this unconsciously by psychic means, I would have had to figure out a year ahead of time that I would become interested in the magnetic field effect and would control the timing of when people did these experiments to get these results.

Mishlove: That's what shamans do, though. They travel back and forth into the future. It's too grandiose for a psychology professor, maybe.

Tart: Definitely.

Mishlove: On the surface, we have a mild-mannered psychology professor here, Charles Tart. If you were to take off your T-shirt, we would see the big shaman emblem. What you're implying, Charley—I don't want to rib you too much about this—is that if viewers are serious about this ESP stuff but find it unreliable, if they begin to pay attention to these subtle environmental factors, there might be ways of augmenting, or even finding some practical value here.

Tart: If somebody wants to use ESP more reliably in their life, there are several things they could do. One would be to keep records of when spontaneous events that they think are ESP happening and take notice of the conditions around them. Do they happen right after a terrible fight, or do they happen on peaceful days? Do they follow meditation periods? You can also obtain the magnetic data.

Mishlove: Where would you obtain it?

Tart: You can get it from the National Oceanographic and Aeronautic Administration. They publish a little bulletin once a month. That's relatively esoteric. I don't think the average viewer will want to do that, but finding whether it correlates with meditation, or your emotional state is very important.

Mishlove: Do you think diet would have an effect?

Tart: I doubt it. I think Americans are crazy about diet. I think we have a national delusion that we can eat our way to enlightenment. Frankly, as a psychologist, I'm far more concerned with the junk food we put in our minds than the junk food we put in our bodies. There may be something to it, but it's not my favorite angle.

Mishlove: Here's another angle. I think Persinger made the claim that very psychic people have had electrical shocks early in their childhood or were electrocuted. Have you heard of that one?

Tart: No, I've never heard of that one. Even if it's true, I would not advise people to go out and get electrical shocks. It's like the idea that some of the very good psychics today got that way by accidentally falling on their heads. Sometimes, that can make people psychic. A lot of times, they just die, so I don't recommend the method at all.

Mishlove: One of your real fields of specialization is the spiritual disciplines. Certainly, in many spiritual traditions, it is said that these disciplines and traditions will lead to the development of various psychic powers, sometimes as a byproduct and sometimes as the goal of the spiritual discipline. How does that jive with the research you've done?

Tart: It doesn't. Looking at relatively psychic people today, you will find the entire spectrum of humanity. You'll find some nasty, neurotic, power-hungry people. You'll find some loving, developed, calm, and spiritual people. You'll find a lot of relatively ordinary people. But I think that's because most of the psychic development we see in the West is accidental, not due to systematically pursuing some spiritual tradition.

As you have said, many Eastern traditions claim that you'll get these psychic abilities automatically as a result of pursuing spiritual disciplines. Unfortunately, we can't check that claim because most of those same traditions have a negative attitude toward psychic abilities.

Mishlove: You're not supposed to demonstrate it.

Tart: You're not supposed to demonstrate it, and you shouldn't even develop it because it's liable to distract you from your goal. That makes it very hard to find out if there's any actual validity to this claim or if it's just an illusion. One of the problems with developing psychic powers is that when you open yourself to the possibility, you may start misinterpreting a lot of ordinary things as psychic abilities. If you're not careful, you can build up a lot of grandiose illusions about the sorts of things you can do.

Mishlove: Conversely, if we look at very successful people—gamblers who win a lot; people who always make good business decisions; people whose lives just seem to be working very well—many of these people have never studied spiritual disciplines. Do you think it's likely that they would perform well on ESP tests?

Tart: I don't know if they would perform well on ESP tests, but I think it's clear that some of them are using ESP. One of the things this illustrates is that there are a lot of very individual roots for this. For one person, practicing a certain kind of yoga might develop their ESP. For another person, playing cards might develop it. At this early stage of our knowledge, it would be a mistake to say that any route is *the* way to develop ESP. It all depends on the person, and it can differ from person to person.

Mishlove: What you're saying is we know very little now.

Tart: I think the feedback principle is relatively universal. In all the various systems for psychic development that seem to work, you'll see that people try something and get some relatively quick feedback about results, and they learn. They realize that if they adopt a certain mental attitude, that seems to make it work at least part of the time, and another mental attitude may never work.

Mishlove: Charley, you've done a lot of research in enhancing or developing psychic abilities. Why is this even important?

Tart: There are possible practical applications for this. We could have a national disaster warning network with a relatively low level of psychic ability, a lot of people, and a way of combining their responses. For instance, impressions from people could be computer analyzed, which might make us say, "There's going to be a big disaster in Ohio in 1992 in the spring. Let's get some emergency supplies there ahead of time." I think that could be developed.

I'm more interested in the implications than the applications. Our world today is in a value crisis. The values that make society tick, and that make an individual's life happy, traditionally come from our religions, but our religions don't work for most people. They are things you were told with no experiential basis that are apparently contradicted by science. So, we're all desperately looking for values. There are a few exceptions, but most people are lost.

The scientific worldview seems to say that all religion is nonsense, and the values that came out of religion are nonsense. For example, in science itself, there's this tremendous tradition that scientists are honest. But if life is just an accidental thing that evolved on this planet because some molecules happened to bump together under the right conditions, and it has no real meaning, why not cheat? I suspect that there's a lot of cheating among second-rate conventional scientists because the morality for not cheating came out of religion.

So, I think it's very important, and this is the thing I'm devoting my life to now: trying to form some bridges for scientifically educated people into the experiential world of spiritual values and spiritual experiences. We can't stay cut off like that. The deep values come from spiritual experiences, not from being told what you should be.

Mishlove: And you see extrasensory perception as being related here?

Tart: I see it as quite related for this reason: Extrasensory perception throws out the "scientistic"—when you make science like a religion—a model of man that says you're nothing but your body and nervous system. That is what we must contend with. The authorities say that all your thoughts, feelings, hopes, and fears are nothing but electrochemical changes going on inside your nervous system. We're isolated from one another, and when you die, that all stops. That's a very depressing worldview.

Now, here's where ESP comes along. The data from parapsychology is not from believers, not from people who say, "I don't like what science says. I was raised to believe the Bible or something, so I will just believe what I feel like. I don't care about the scientific method." The data in parapsychology comes from people who have used the scientific method extremely well and have found that the very existence of ESP means you can no longer say the mind is nothing but the brain and body. It says that the mind is something bigger than the brain and body.

Mishlove: Isn't that still an open question?

Tart: It's not an open question.

Mishlove: You think it's clear.

Tart: I'll go on record as being closed-minded, I suppose.

Mishlove: But in effect, your research with the geomagnetic fields suggests a physical basis.

Tart: Let's put it this way. Some people want to scientifically quarrel about whether there's enough evidence to believe in ESP. I think there's something wrong there. There's an overwhelming amount of very high-quality scientific evidence for the existence of several versions of ESP.

Mishlove: I wouldn't doubt that for a minute, but then others might say, given all this evidence, we'll accept that there still might be a materialistic interpretation of it all.

Tart: Oh yes, but that is a particular religious doctrine known as promissory materialism. We promise you that someday in the future, it'll all be explained in the laboratory. That's not a decent scientific theory because, by the very rules of science, you can't falsify it. You can never prove that someday there won't be an explanation that comes out of the laboratory. That's an act of faith.

Mishlove: That's the act of faith that scientists make all the time.

Tart: Most of them make it, but they don't have to. Faith can become experimental and empirical. You don't have to just blindly believe in anything. I think faith should be experimental. You should try believing in things, observe the consequences on yourself, and then step back and see what happens.

Mishlove: To return to your original point, you feel that ESP is something that scientists can do to develop this kind of experimental faith.

Tart: Not just scientists. Most people in our culture have been strongly affected or rejected by the results of science. You don't have to be a scientist to have had your consciousness shaped by this religion of scientism. This is relevant to almost any educated person that we don't know that the mind equals the brain. The mind does things we cannot reduce to brain functioning. That doesn't prove that any religion is true, but it makes you open-minded toward all our spiritual traditions. That open-mindedness toward our spiritual traditions is vital in our world today.

Mishlove: I suppose an insight like that got you started on your own journey many years ago.

Tart: It was part of it, yes. During my own adolescence, I struggled with this conflict between science and religion. I was raised in a traditional faith as a child and believed it. As I got to be an adolescent, I started learning a lot about science and saw all these incompatible things. It was interesting. I saw what a lot of my contemporaries did, and they took one of two routes: they simply accepted that science explained religious beliefs, or they did a little psychological defense maneuver we might call compartmentalization. There is more prestige in being scientific rather than religious as well. Religion was moved to 11 o'clock on Sunday mornings, at which time they "believed" and never thought about it for the rest of the week.

As a psychologist, I know compartmentalization isn't a healthy way of organizing your world. I was lucky. I was doing a lot of reading at the time, and I stumbled upon parapsychology literature. Some people had struggled with the same conflict between science and religion and said, "Okay, let's neither believe nor disbelieve. Let's do open-minded experiments and find out what, in this vast area we might call religious or spiritual, has some basis for it and what is indeed superstition. Let's separate the wheat from the chaff." That motivation has been with me ever since.

Mishlove: It seems as if you've done that quite well, Charley. You've been able to integrate many different worlds as a transpersonal psychologist, a parapsychologist, a professor, and, for my money, a shaman as well.

Tart: Thank you.

Mishlove: Charley, it's been a pleasure having you with me this evening. Thank you very much.

4

Cultivating Mindfulness

~

Recorded in 1996

Jeffrey Mishlove: Hello and welcome. I'm Jeffrey Mishlove. Today, we're going to be discussing the cultivation of mindfulness. With me is Dr. Charles Tart, a professor of psychology at the University of California at Davis.

Welcome, Charley.

Charles Tart: Good evening, Jeffrey.

Mishlove: It's a pleasure to have you here. When we think of the problems of modern life, everything from ecology to our social and political problems to our economic and military problems, it strikes me that a lack of mindfulness or mindlessness might be the root cause of virtually all these conditions.

Tart: That's an excellent way of thinking about it. It's as if we're dreaming. When we dream at night, a wonderful safety system cuts in where a part of the brain paralyzes us so we can't talk, we can't act, and so forth. We can have these fantasies—being out of touch with reality—with no consequences. But in everyday life, we can be very mindless and caught up in our daydreams, projections, hopes, and fears and act on them. That's where the problem comes from. We act out our fantasies.

Mishlove: It's as if the fundamental premises upon which all our actions are based are ultimately somehow mythological. We have so many things we assume.

Tart: Yes, each of us is walking around lost in our personal myth, which interacts with our cultural myth, which interacts with our world myth. As a result, we don't perceive things the way they are. The East had this idea long before we did when they talked about living in *maya* or *samsara:* in a state of illusion. It's not that the world isn't real—it's that we're so immersed in our daydreams, hopes, and fears that we distort our perceptions. That's what gets us into trouble.

Mishlove: The irony of it is that when we try to be rational, when we try to think about the problem, is when we get ourselves into the greatest trouble.

Tart: Thinking won't solve it. It's not just that we're not thinking right— that's part of it. The problem is that we're not perceiving correctly. In a sense, our automatic thoughts are taking over our perceptions and distorting them. An intellectual analysis is fine as a starting place, but then you've got to learn the skill of being present in the moment, of seeing, hearing, and tasting things the way they are.

Mishlove: In other words, getting in touch with raw experience underneath the cognitive layer of how we think of things.

Tart: Right, living here and now. This is especially important in our interactions with other people. So many times, two people may be having a conversation—like we are now, for instance—and I have my myth of who I am, and you have a certain role in my mythology. You have your myth of who I am, and I have a minor role in that. Each of us is lost in our myth and not noticing what the other person is feeling or communicating. Naturally, that's going to make for a funny kind of relationship. Psychological studies have shown that this is the norm. It's extremely common for people to be lost in their projections when they think they're relating to how other people are.

Mishlove: It would seem to me that there's no getting out of it. We all have a concept of what it means to be human. It would seem to me that, ultimately, nobody knows.

Tart: But if you reach the conclusion that nobody knows, that's liable to stop you from trying. I'd rather say that I don't know the limits on being present and realistic, except they're a lot better than what we normally do. So, let's not worry about ultimate limits. Let's get on with becoming mindful.

It reminds me of a story that's attributed to the Buddha: a man was shot with a poisoned arrow. Another traveler comes along and says he will pull it out. The wounded man says, "Wait a minute, there are some important things we must figure out first. Like, who shot this arrow? What was his motivation? Who provided him with the poison? Why is there a society that allows things like this to happen?" In the meantime, the poison is spreading. It's interesting to think about the causes and the ultimate possibilities. But we need to get to work coming to our senses, finding out what's going on now, and asking the ultimate questions.

Mishlove: When you say coming to our senses, I gather you mean that in a literal way.

Tart: Yes, I mean it in a very literal way. Most of the time, we focus a small percentage of our attention on what our senses perceive. Then, they are immediately abstracted into thoughts, concepts, beliefs, and prejudices. Those are the things we're aware of. For instance, I may walk down the street and see a rose bush. After a fraction of a second of seeing it, the concept of a rose as a beautiful flower with a nice smell dominates my mind. I mechanically bend over and sniff it, but I'm not paying attention to that actual rose. I'm lost in my concepts about it. It is a non-nourishing experience compared to noticing this rose's scent and color.

Mishlove: Why is it that we can't, or don't, normally just have the intense, sensual experience of a real rose? Why is it that the concept pops up in our minds instead?

Tart: It's because abstraction is very useful. We live in a complicated world where we can't handle all the sensory data in all its rich detail. We have immediate goals. What's wrong with abstraction is that it becomes automatic, running all the time.

Mishlove: From a psychological perspective, our problem is that we are intermittently reinforced for using abstract thoughts.

Tart: That's a good way to put it. We get into the habit, but it goes even further than that. We automatically create thoughts and distorted perceptions that satisfy us and cause us to withdraw from the reality of the world, which seems good. You can withdraw from some of the pain in the world because you're too busy with your own thoughts. The trouble is that in the long run, you pay an extremely high price for that kind of withdrawal because you do stupid things in the world. You generate negative karma in an Eastern sense by acting maladaptively.

For instance, if we're having a conversation, and I'm wrapped up in my personal beliefs about you and don't notice the actual you, at some level, you will notice and resent it. I may act in inappropriate ways, and you're going to retaliate in some way. Or I'm just going to do stupid things that don't fit the situation, and we end up with more suffering, which then tempts us to work harder on our projections, so we don't notice that pain. It becomes a vicious spiral.

Mishlove: You seem to tell the story of modern culture in many ways. Certainly, if we look at literature and theater, this kind of failure of people to encounter each other is a major theme of modern existence.

Tart: I don't know that it's at all limited to modern culture, but I'll say this about modern culture: we have more technological tools for distracting ourselves than any other culture has ever had. You can sit in front of the television all day. You can get either legal or illegal drugs, which will cut you off from reality. The diversions available to prime fantasies are innumerable today.

Mishlove: At the same time, we have developed communication technologies that connect us with many cultures worldwide and overcome this issue.

Tart: That's right. We have mindfulness techniques from all over the planet that are designed to create greater awareness of reality. We have ideas that have come in from other cultures, and we now must adapt them to our culture. It's fine to realize that we're not fully aware much of the time. What usually happens is you figure that out a year later, the stupid thing you said that you weren't aware of at the time. Well, a year later, it may be too late to do anything about it. What you want to do is be aware of what you're doing now, and if it's inappropriate, stop it. This is where mindfulness techniques are very helpful.

For the past couple of years, I've been learning what, for me, is a new kind of mindfulness technique, which is classical meditation. I call it classical because it's generally recommended that you sit in a quiet place where you won't be interrupted by the telephone or other distractions. You start looking at how your mind operates, which can be horrible in a sense because what so many of us discover is that our mind is out of control.

Mishlove: Just racing, racing, racing.

Tart: Yes. I think I'm going to sit there and be calm and just be aware of the sensations in my body, but my mind says, "Hey, that's a good idea. I could write a paper about that. Let's see, what's the most interesting sense? No, wait a minute. I wanted to sit here and be aware of my sensations." So, you discover that your thoughts race. Eventually, with practice, you learn not to be carried away by racing thoughts, fantasies, and dreams. You become mindful of what you feel like and that's very rewarding. I'm just beginning to taste that, in a sense, to just *be* instead of producing and thinking. It also leads to very interesting insights that can be useful in everyday life.

Mishlove: When you talk about classical meditation, what do you have in mind?

Tart: An excellent example would be Buddhist Vipassana or insight meditation. There are variations of this meditation around the world. You're told to sit and witness what's going on, observing without trying to change anything. You learn a lot from that. For instance, it is hard not to change things, and you have preferences. Well, this sensation in my body doesn't strike me as special or spiritual. I'm here to have a spiritual experience. No, you said you were there to observe whatever happens. So, you learn a lot about the biases that affect your life and so forth.

But I found a problem with this, and I've noticed it in other people doing these classical-style meditations: you don't live there in a nice, quiet place. Most of your life is spent out where people talk to you, the phone rings, and events happen. It's very hard to maintain mindfulness in those kinds of situations.

Mishlove: I recall a story about a man who studied for nine years in a Buddhist monastery and mastered this kind of meditation. When he left the monastery, he immediately went out into the world, got married, and had a horrible marriage. He remarked that his experience as a meditator did not prepare him at all for dealing with real-world issues.

Tart: One of the problems in adapting the Eastern techniques to our culture is that they're very monastic-oriented techniques in a lot of ways. It is real life for a monk or a nun to sit in a quiet place to meditate or perform a slow-walking meditation. But I don't think this kind of monastic tradition will be compatible with our culture for most people. We need mindfulness that can be carried into our everyday lives. Can I be mindful when I'm talking here with TV cameras on me, not just when I'm sitting in a quiet room by myself?

Mishlove: Or hooked up to biofeedback.

Tart: That's right.

Mishlove: Are there such skills or traditions in this direction?

Tart: I wrote a lot about this in my *Waking Up* book, drawing especially on Gurdjieff's teachings about developing mindfulness in everyday life.

Mishlove: I suppose athletic training might be another example of that.

Tart: Yes, that tends to be a specialized kind of mindfulness, though. Learn how to move your body in a certain optimal way. Almost any kind of skill training is specialized mindfulness training.

Mishlove: such as musical training.

Tart: When you get a skill down well, it becomes automatic, and the mindfulness of it is lost, which can be an advantage in some ways because habitual behaviors are faster than your conscious awareness. But then, if change is needed, it can be a real block when something is automated. Gurdjieff's idea was more a matter of learning to develop a simultaneous witnessing consciousness as part of your everyday life: while you wash the dishes, while you open the door, while you talk to someone, while you go to the bathroom, in all kinds of everyday things.

Mishlove: Who is Gurdjieff?

Tart: Gurdjieff was one of the first people to try to adapt Eastern ideas about mindfulness to Western culture, beginning around the turn of the 20th century. He died in the 1940s, and many groups still operate on his principles of being mindful as part of everyday life. There's a very complex philosophy that goes along with it. He told people they were walking around in a dangerous daydream. For instance, you can sign checks even though you're not aware that you're doing it. He taught people to be aware of what's happening in the moment. How does your body feel? What are your emotions? What are you perceiving? What's your physical position in this situation? It's a very useful skill.

Mishlove: Let's suppose you were to ask me how I am. I might have an automatic answer such as "Oh, I'm just fine," as people normally do in our culture. Mindfulness would stop that process to get underneath it somehow.

Tart: Suppose I ask you, "Who are you?" and ask you to reply mindfully.

Mishlove: It was a little funny.

Tart: Yes, but I'm asking you to be mindful at this moment.

Mishlove: Who am I? I don't know that I have a name when I'm being mindful. A name has so much baggage associated with it.

Tart: That's wonderful. You touched your identity for a moment, and then you had a very clever thought that took you away from the mindfulness again.

Mishlove: I was going to say, "Who am I? I'm me." I don't know if that's an automatic reply.

Tart: I think you had a taste, for a moment, of that mental machinery stopping, and a whole universe can open when you stop it. Some meditation techniques try to forcefully stop the mental machinery using a sudden shock or sudden change of conditions, leaving you without your automatic games, habits, and filters for a moment. You're back to something much more basic that's behind all the other stuff, anyway.

Gurdjieff's work tries to do that in ordinary life, whereas meditative traditions do it in a special, quiet setting. My experience has been that cultivating mindfulness in everyday life is very useful, and you learn a lot about yourself. You don't learn too much about deep fundamental aspects of yourself because you're too busy. In everyday life, there's a lot of stuff coming in, grabbing our attention. In the meditative traditions, on the other hand, you've eliminated all that heavy outside stimulation, so you see many of the more subtle things about yourself. What I'm interested in now is not only learning the meditative practices better myself. They're very interesting, and there's a lot of psychology involved with them, but I want to bridge the gap. How do you go from the meditative state to everyday life, and then from everyday life to the meditative state, maintaining mindfulness over a wide variety of conditions?

Mishlove: As I reflect on the experience, I just had with you, I feel a lot of vulnerability. Really becoming mindful means letting go of a lot of things that I associate with my adult self and becoming childlike in some ways, and that's a bit frightening.

Tart: One of the things that happens to all of us to some degree as children is that our true selves are attacked, invalidated, and denied, and we create a persona, a false personality. Gurdjieff's wonderful term for it was to protect ourselves, which is a somewhat conscious act, to begin with, but it all becomes automatic. Mindfulness is to be in that reality as a small child who hasn't grown up yet and feels vulnerable. You must be kind to yourself in this process. You don't show that vulnerability in a situation where you might get hurt, for instance. Part of being mindful is knowing what's possible in each situation.

Mishlove: I need to be mindful in a way to know that this baggage is part of me in some way. If I need to use it in an appropriate situation, I need to be assertive.

Tart: The point of Gurdjieff's work—and I see this as the point of some of the classical meditations—is to develop a new center of the self that is not the ordinary ego. It's the center of oneself that has infinite possibilities, doesn't identify with anything, and is very aware. You can use all the ordinary aspects of your personality as tools when they're appropriate but then put them away when they're not appropriate. Ordinarily, our false personalities just run on automatic; they don't stop. We identify better with them and fight to save them, so the mindfulness traditions invite us to take chances and drop the habit. Fortunately, you get a fair amount of very positive experiences as a reward for doing that, but there are certainly moments when it's frightening.

Mishlove: We cling so much to our egos and often identify with them. If I think of the ego, I think of the part of me that considers myself separate from you and everything else. That's the part that you're talking about letting go of.

Tart: Our egos act like armor in a way that keeps us separate and defended. I was hurt once upon a time by somebody outside myself, so I'm going to close myself off. I've built a wall of skills, anecdotes, verbal plays, and personality characteristics around me to protect that vulnerability. We're not tiny children anymore and not at the mercy of other people. We can let those defenses down in our minds and look at the world more open-mindedly.

Mishlove: You talked about developing a new center of the self, which is not the ego.

Tart: I feel ambivalent about using the term "center" because even using it "thingifies" it and makes it a little too concrete. With mindfulness training, you develop a shift toward a process. It's better to say instead of this thing being the precious, unchangeable me, it's rather more like you flow with all sorts of things.

Mishlove: One becomes the dance rather than the dancer.

Tart: Yes. One goes from dancer to the dance and moves to other situations. It's flexible, leading to great creativity in life and making it easier to deal with things.

Mishlove: Are there processes for cultivating this different sensibility, or is it just a question of one cultivating mindfulness by being mindful?

Tart: Yes, some skilled beings can be helpful. Working with more mindful people can remind you when you've lost it, for instance. You can tell people just to be generally mindful, and that's great, but it's kind of vague and abstract, or you can be mindful in more specific ways. For example, every time you come to a door today, open it with the opposite hand, then you're bringing some deliberate mindfulness into a very specific situation that people can work with.

Mishlove: In other words, breaking habits.

Tart: Not that breaking the habit is necessary, but the effort to be aware and do it differently helps create the kind of mindfulness you need.

Mishlove: One of the traps that we fall into is that we may have perfectly good habits, but we're unaware that we have them.

Tart: This is where meditation and mindfulness practice are very revealing because you discover these habits. Normally, I open doors with my right hand, and I realized, at the end of the day, though I intended to use my left hand, I didn't remember once to open a door with my left hand. I've learned a few things. I've got a strong habit of using my right hand to open doors, and I have very little capacity to be mindful, even though I said I would be. Learning that is a great step. That might motivate me to work harder. There are lots of specific techniques for moving toward ultimate mindfulness. I wrote about several classical meditative procedures in the *Waking Up* book. They're a means toward greater mindfulness.

Mishlove: Often in our culture, we hear the term consciousness-raising. I wonder how you would distinguish between consciousness-raising or consciousness and mindfulness.

Tart: What consciousness-raising usually means in practice is when I get you to agree with my point of view. It's become politicized. Mindfulness goes beyond accepting or rejecting a particular viewpoint; it's about being present to who you are now, to the world you're in, your position in it, and your feelings. It involves more freedom of action to decide what's best instead of just being swept along by habit. Reaching what the classical traditions call enlightenment or awakening is where you discover more about your true nature instead of always being swept downstream by your mental and emotional habits.

Mishlove: You suggest that this quality of mindfulness or presence is almost independent of one's political, religious, or scientific beliefs.

Tart: Let me put it this way. What's the best form of government in an insane asylum? Should it be a democracy, socialism, or a monarchy? Any of those choices are silly. If the people are insane, no matter what form of government, they will mess things up. What you need in an insane asylum is to bring people to sanity. Most of our social forms would work excellently if we had people awake to the present moment instead of people who are conditioned by habit.

Mishlove: Charley Tart, it's been a pleasure having you with me. You're performing a very valuable service by introducing such a fundamental concept as mindfulness into the world of psychology and into our society.

Tart: I think we can end by asking everyone to take a moment to reflect on "Who am I?"

Mishlove: Charley, thank you very much for being with me.

Tart: My pleasure, Jeffrey.

5

Six Decades in Parapsychology

~

Recorded on November 9, 2016

Jeffrey Mishlove: Hello and welcome. I'm Jeffrey Mishlove. Today, we'll be exploring six decades in parapsychology. With me is my old friend and mentor, Dr. Charles Tart, who is an emeritus professor of psychology at the University of California at Davis and the Institute of Transpersonal Psychology. Dr. Tart was one of my faculty committee members when I was a graduate student in parapsychology at the University of California. He is the author of numerous books and over a hundred scientific papers in parapsychology. His books include the classic *Altered States of Consciousness*, an anthology; *States of Consciousness, Psi: Scientific Studies of the Psychic Realm*, as well as *Learning to Use Extrasensory Perception*. Welcome, Charley.

Charles Tart: Good to be here, Jeff.

Mishlove: It's a pleasure to be with you. I want to acknowledge the important role that you've had in inspiring and guiding me to pursue my career in parapsychology.

Tart: I don't know how much I inspired you. You were self-propelled. I could give you useful information, but I didn't have to motivate you to do something.

Mishlove: It was at a distance. You were a pioneer long before I got into the field and already famous before I got started. I think our readers would like to know what brought you into the field of parapsychology. How has it gone for the last six decades?

Tart: Some of my friends have kidded me that I'm basically trying to figure out how my mother did it. Almost everybody I know had the experience as a kid where you're alone somewhere in the house, and you're doing something that you probably shouldn't be doing. Then you hear from the other end of the house your mother calling, "What are you doing?" How did she know? I asked her if she read my mind, and she'd say, "Of course." As a parent, I know that if children are quiet, they're up to something.

I also had a conventional religious background. My grandmother, who had unconditional love for me, would take me to Sunday school and church. If it was good enough for my grandmother, it was good enough for me. Then, during my teenage years, I began to read about science extensively. I was in love with everything scientific, and I realized that a lot of what science said was the truth about the world. However, it conflicted with what religion said was true. I also noticed that adults were hypocritical, too, in terms of doing what they preached for you to do. I was getting more alienated from my religion while becoming more in love with science but feeling something was wrong. There is clearly a lot of good stuff associated with religion. God bless the Trenton Public Library; they had a lot of old books on psychical research, as parapsychology was originally called.

Mishlove: Trenton, New Jersey.

Tart: Trenton, New Jersey, yes. I realized from reading psychical books that this wasn't just my problem, but something that a lot of intelligent people had dealt with starting in the 1800s when science had become a powerful force in society. People were horrified that religion was being totally thrown out; where would our values come from in that case? They got the idea that the scientific method had worked very well in learning about things when applied in the physical world. Could we take the scientific method—the essence of good observation and logical thinking—and apply it to phenomena associated with religion and spirituality?

That has been the central theme of my career since my teenage years, where in my teenage years it was mostly reading about it. Then it's been active experiments in many ways, writing, thinking, and so forth. How can I take the essence of science and use it to clarify what's there in spirituality? I'm going to talk about spirituality now, because I understand that spirituality means somebody has some overwhelming experience and they start talking about it, and soon there are committees that turn what they experienced into doctrine, and then you get into the whole sociology of religion, which I'm no expert on. But there are experiences people have, like near-death experiences, that have profound spiritual implications for people. How much of that is based on reality? Conviction alone isn't enough. Just because you experience something very intensely and it's obviously *the* truth, well, that's what you experience, don't not count that, but that doesn't necessarily mean it's true about the world. So yes, parapsychology for 70 years now, from my teenage years on.

Mishlove: What drew you specifically into parapsychology research, because combining religion and science could have brought you into philosophy or religious studies or just conventional psychology? Something drew you to the paranormal.

Tart: Well, the drawing to the science part of it was partly that I loved gadgets. I was a ham radio operator. I learned so much about electronics that I was able to pass federal tests for a first-class radiotelephone license and work my way through college working at radio stations and the like. So, science had gadgets. That was important. As I got a little older in life, too, I learned that talk is cheap, and I learned it the hard way. For instance, in my thirties I got interested in the Japanese martial art of aikido and arranged for a black belt instructor to come up to UC Davis and teach it. I was the advisor to the student club, so I got to train in it, too. I discovered in about three weeks that I could explain the martial art of aikido much better than my black belt instructor. He only had a high school education. I could compare it to philosophy and scientific developments and physiology and all that, except I kept noticing I couldn't do anything, and he could toss me across the room with his little finger. Something was not computing here. It took me years to realize there was a different kind of knowledge there, and just talking good is not enough. I think I had a black belt in talking by the time I was twelve, and that's nice in some ways, but part of my main spiritual and psychological growth discipline in life is to not be carried away by clever talking, even when I'm the person doing the clever talking.

Mishlove: You got associated with Dr. Andrija Puharich back in the 1950s. He had the Round Table Foundation, as I recall, up in Maine. Puharich is known these days mostly, I suppose, for his discovery of Uri Geller, the Israeli psychic, but back in those days he had an active research program, and you became an associate of his.

Tart: Yeah, in 1953 I went off to college, MIT. I thought I was going to be an engineer. That was ended by math, which I don't have that much of a talent for. Being in Boston, I went to several lectures by parapsychologists, including Puharich. Eileen Garrett, particularly, that world-famous medium who started the Parapsychology Foundation, talked about the research support they had given Puharich and that he had an electrical technique which could amplify extrasensory perception. And of course, that got me excited. An electrical gadget? I understood electrical gadgets. The problem with ESP research was that when you try to study it in the laboratory, it's generally so weak and unreliable that it doesn't happen too much of the time. It happens enough to show that it's real, but you can't produce it on demand, and then it's liable to be kind of statistically significant, but it doesn't convince you that something real is happening.

We had a psychic research club that we had founded. We had Puharich come down and talk. I was fascinated enough by what he'd done to say, "I need a summer job to earn money for college. You've got a position open?" He had a research assistant position open. I earned a dollar an hour, which I thought was good back then.

Mishlove: Yeah, back in those days.

Tart: Dollar an hour and room and board. Hey, that was all right. So, I spent the summer at his private research foundation in Maine. That was charming. It was charming because it was a beautiful place. I'd never been to Maine before. It was an old mansion on the coast. The taxes had become too much for rich people to keep, so they gave it to charitable places. We had all sorts of interesting psychics visit. Morey Bernstein, the guy who wrote *The Search for Bridey Murphy*, was there a lot. Peter Hurkos, the European psychic, was there. But I was especially interested in the Faraday cage research that was supposed to help ESP.

Now, a Faraday cage. Your car is a kind of inefficient Faraday cage. It's inefficient because it has a lot of openings. If it was a solid metal box, then if you were struck by lightning on the outside, but you were inside this solid metal box, you wouldn't feel a thing. It's the property of this kind of electrically conducting box that all the electricity stays on the outside. That's interesting.

Mishlove: So, you're shielded.

Tart: You're shielded. Yes, you're very thoroughly shielded from anything.

Mishlove: The idea for parapsychology research, I suppose, is that it prevents any kind of electromagnetic signal from being the source of ESP, if ESP is evident.

Tart: That was important for a few people, but I think by then there was already more than enough evidence to show that whatever ESP is, it's not electromagnetic. It doesn't fall off with distance, for instance. You can't detect it with radio receivers. But it's an interesting and scientific-looking environment. Puharich made all sorts of experiments with Faraday cages. His two most basic findings were that, if your Faraday cage was electrically insulated from ground—he had a six-foot metal cube with a door in it and it sat on glass blocks, which does not conduct electricity. If you tried to do an ESP test with one person inside that way and another person outside somewhere, they generally scored at chance. It's like this electrically floating, as it was technically described, Faraday cage blocked ESP. But if you connected the Faraday cage to the earth, to a six-foot rod driven into moist ground, ESP was better than under ordinary room conditions. He had an amplifier, and he had a shield, and that was exciting. He had a third condition, too, where you pumped this Faraday cage up to about 5,000 volts with respect to ground, which also amplified ESP, but that was getting a little too exciting.

Mishlove: You independently replicated some of these studies later.

Tart: Many years later. I replicated the basic one. There were many variations that I didn't have a chance to do. The thing that was lacking in Puharich's work was that it wasn't double-blind. That is, if you know that somebody is doing something special for you in an experiment, that could psychologically alone change your performance. Puharich knew when he was changing these conditions, the subjects often knew. But I was able to do it years later where the experimenters and the subjects did not know what the electrical conditions were. I didn't have the advantage Puharich had of having subjects to work with who already could demonstrate significant ESP scores in matching tests under room conditions. I had to use college students, but these were highly motivated people in my experimental psychology class, and we got the effect. When my Faraday cage was electrically floating, they scored at chance, and when it was grounded, they scored above chance. It was a small score, but it was big enough to be statistically significant. I figured I had basically replicated it.

Now, this goes on to the crazy part. Even back in 1957 when I worked for him, I said, why isn't every parapsychologist in the world, all dozen or two dozen of them, doing this same sort of research? Because if we could amplify ESP, we'd take a huge step forward. I used to use the analogy that our understanding of ESP then was like humanity's understanding of electricity had been for practically all human history. You had lightning flashes, and it was all over. You had memories to work with which might be accurate or inaccurate and so forth. We have these deathbed visions and things like that, but you can't get very far with that. You also had static electrical effects. Sometimes, if you rubbed a glass rod with some fur, you might be able to pick up a feather, and it didn't always work. You had these very weak, unreliable effects. That's what our laboratory effects are like.

Mishlove: Up until Ben Franklin came along.

Tart: And showed that lightning was indeed electricity. But what changed was when the Italian Volta invented an electrical battery. Now, it was nothing compared to lightning, but it was a steady electrical current and you could experiment with the properties of electricity. In no time at all on the human history time scale we have video, audio, and all this wonderful stuff. We need the ESP battery. It looked like the Faraday cage could do it, but nobody else was replicating it.

Mishlove: After half a century, you're the only one who even tried to replicate that study.

Tart: That's right.

Mishlove: Puharich published a book long ago called *Beyond Telepathy*. In that book he argued that if you're in a very relaxed neurological state—I think he called it the cholinergic state—that increased your receptivity for ESP. If you're aroused in an adrenergic state, then you're a better telepathic sender.

Tart: And nobody's ever replicated that either.

Mishlove: But it does seem to correlate well with the anecdotal literature. I think there have been many studies correlating relaxation techniques, hypnosis, meditation, and so on.

Tart: The anecdotal literature that it would fit with well is, you're in the process of being horribly murdered, so you're aroused in an adrenergic state. Your mother, a thousand miles away, is asleep and she's very relaxed in a cholinergic state and she has a dream in which you appear. But again, that's a little hard to experiment with.

Mishlove: It is, but it's one of the most reported spontaneous experiences that people have.

Tart: But the sender has been neglected in parapsychological research. I think part of the reason for that was that telepathy made a certain kind of sense to people. If I'm attempting to communicate something to you, maybe I'm sending out radio waves or quantum stuff or something. But [with] clairvoyance, here's a deck of cards in a box. Write down what the order is. Nobody has looked at these cards since they've been shuffled. Nobody's sending. It's not known to anybody. It turned out that, at least in most of the laboratory studies, clairvoyance works just as well as telepathy experiments. Maybe this person trying to send it doesn't matter. So, the sender has been extremely neglected, and I suspect that's a loss.

Mishlove: As you look back now over more than six decades in the field, what is your reflection? Was it worthwhile?

Tart: Oh, yes. I mean, I ran into a lot of trouble for daring to be interested in taboo subjects, but it was very exciting. We're not up to the stage where our knowledge of the spiritual and the psychic sense is so advanced that we can say [that] prayers by Baptists are answered more often than prayers by Buddhists. I don't know if we'll ever get to that stage. But there is enough evidence that I feel I can say quite confidently as a scientist that the human mind is more than the human brain; that the mind can sometimes reach out. We can call it telepathy if people seem to be intending to reach it. It can sometimes reach out and just pick up information about distant things. Call it clairvoyance. Sometimes [it can] reach into the future and correctly identify stuff that hasn't even been determined yet. The evidence for that is overwhelming. I hate it. Precognition makes no sense at all to me. I think now is now and the future hasn't happened yet, but the evidence compels me as a scientist to say it happens.

Mishlove: Didn't you also do, if I remember correctly, a very interesting study showing that precognition scores fall off the further distant in time the target is?

Tart: I did do such a study and then later somebody pointed out a possible flaw in it, so I added a note to it saying don't take this too seriously. It makes it seem more like physical stuff that we know, that the greater the distance the less it should work. I don't know that that's true and I wasn't motivated to do that. The main reason I must accept clairvoyance is in some of my own research on ordinary telepathy—present time stuff, somebody now is sending, somebody now is trying to receive—I discovered massive amounts of strong precognition effects that gave some clues as to how ESP may work as an information carrying system. I was shocked, but there it was in my own laboratory data, very strong.

Mishlove: You've published, to my recollection, well over a hundred scientific papers in parapsychology.

Tart: Yeah, a couple hundred. I'm proud of that. In parapsychology, no, we'll probably go back to a hundred there because I only give about a third of my time to parapsychology.

Mishlove: You were also very active in transpersonal psychology, and you wrote a fascinating book called *The End of Materialism* in which you basically use the data of parapsychology to argue for, I guess, what would be a dualist philosophical perspective. You're saying we cannot explain this data using a materialistic metaphysical framework.

Tart: Right, that's what I was starting to talk about when I said thinking the mind is nothing, but the brain is just factually incorrect. We don't know how a brain can produce consciousness in the first place, although people promise it. Philosophers long ago named this promissory materialism. "Someday they'll explain it in terms of the brain functioning." We can't disprove that. "Someday they'll explain it in terms of little green men and big flying saucers." You can't disprove that statement either, but I wouldn't hold my breath waiting for it. Here the mind has got three ways of getting information about things at a distance and things in the future, and the mind can sometimes by intention alone reach out and change things, psychokinesis or telekinesis. Well, that sounds like a mind then for instance that maybe could survive the death of the body.

Now, we're a long way from checking the reality of heaven. I don't know what the ultimate limits are, but I now tend to look at all religions, and especially the purer spiritual traditions behind them, as people had things happen some of which were real psychic phenomena, and they've come up with explanations for them which turn into religious doctrines. That's where the science stops. Fortunately, in science you must understand, your explanation is always subject to retesting and change. Many a wonderful theory has had an inconvenient fact come along and die quickly. But religions turn into doctrines, and you must not question this, or you'll go to hell. That to me is a real inhibition of our spiritual possibilities because I think we can learn so much more about this spiritual aspect of human beings.

Mishlove: It's largely establishment academics and establishment scientists who feel threatened by parapsychology. But what you're saying is that it also has implications for the theologians of various religions.

Tart: I suspect theologians are even more resistant than academics because, by the time you become a theologian in a particular tradition, you know some doctrine inside and out and part of your job is defending and clarifying that doctrine. You don't welcome something that simply may not do that. Let me give you an example. This is something we should have a lot of data on, but we have only just one small beginning of it. In Buddhism they believe in reincarnation. That's okay. We have a lot of kids who remember previous lives. That's very interesting material. I'm not sure there is reincarnation but let's assume it happens. There's another doctrine in Buddhism that says it's extremely difficult to be reincarnated as a human being. You must be very spiritually advanced, have very good karma to do that and not be reincarnated as an animal or in some other realm and so forth. So hardly anybody gets reincarnated as a human being, maybe once every thousand incarnations.

Mishlove: I know the Buddha himself talks about his previous incarnations as animals.

Tart: Right, and then they were all humans for a while. That's an interesting doctrine. I made a prediction from that. I said my colleagues at the University of Virginia have several thousand cases now of kids who remember previous lives. How many of those previous lives were people that we would think would be spiritually advanced? Monks and nuns and yogis and so forth. I got them scratching their heads. They hadn't thought of looking at that but there might be two or three among several thousand. Well, that doesn't support the idea that you've got to have that kind of karma to be reincarnated as a human.

Mishlove: Nor am I aware of any case where a young child remembers having been an animal in a previous lifetime.

Tart: No, I don't remember that either. I think the jump to being a human being is so different from being an animal that it's hard to imagine going back. This is very speculative but I'm speculating on where we could go if we build up a solid bunch of data about this stuff.

Mishlove: If you look to the future of parapsychology, I think you're suggesting we may be able eventually to answer the kind of questions that spiritual seekers are asking.

Tart: I'll say answer, but I'll qualify "answer." Most people say we'll get an answer that it's now 100 percent certain that things are this way. A lot of spiritual stuff I don't think you'll ever be 100 percent certain one way or the other, but now most spiritual ideas have one percent evidence, and the rest is all belief. I would much rather have some spiritual beliefs that had a lot of evidence in favor of them rather than none. The conclusion I drew from my book, *End of Materialism*—would apply to people in general because this was written for people in general, not for parapsychologists—is the idea that science has totally disproven the spiritual is false. Mainstream science has ignored the spiritual or condemned it out of hand for philosophical reasons, but it has not been disproved.

Mishlove: Or been condemned by spiritual authorities.

Tart: Yeah. Second, the idea that there may be some reality to spiritual effects is supported by parapsychology, again which many of my colleagues don't like because they want to make it more like physics because there'll be less opposition that way. It's reasonable to be both scientific and spiritually inclined in your life. You still need to exercise lots of discrimination in both those areas because there's nonsense all over the place, but you're not automatically crazy just because you think there's something to the spiritual. A lot of people have been taught that and suffered a great deal because of it and it's a real shame.

Mishlove: Dr. Charles Tart, what a pleasure to have this half hour with you. Thank you.

Tart: Thank you, Jeff.

6

Learning to Use Extrasensory Perception

~

Recorded on November 9, 2016

Jeffrey Mishlove: Our topic today is cultivating extrasensory perception. With me is Dr. Charles Tart who was a faculty member on my dissertation committee at the University of California. I wrote *Psi Development Systems* which was based on my doctoral dissertation. Welcome, Charley.

Charles Tart: Welcome Jeffrey. I'm getting tired hearing all those titles.

Mishlove: And I haven't mentioned them all. You've had an illustrious career, and, in a way, you threaded the needle maintaining an academic position for all those decades while you rigorously researched taboo topics. In your book, *Learning to Use Extrasensory Perception,* you specifically focus on the important question of feedback as a learning tool. So, let's start there.

Tart: Suppose Jeffrey, that I ask you to hold your hand out, palm flat, and while contracting your index finger to start turning your hand back and forth 180 degrees. Now put that down and read my mind. At first, I asked you to do a small variation on a talent you're already exquisitely skilled at, controlling the movements of your hand. Then I asked you to do something unfamiliar. We have somebody come in for an experiment and we tell them that somebody's thinking of something in another room, read their mind or read the order of this deck of cards in a sealed box.

Mishlove: Like "How am I supposed to do that?"

Tart: Yeah. Should I squint? Should I relax? Should I pray? It's not something you already know how to do. Very few people already have some controllable ESP skill.

Mishlove: When you're working with college students, typically they're not experienced.

Tart: That's right, they're very inexperienced in ESP. Almost all the tests of ESP that have been done previously have been based on a model that used somebody with a certain level of ESP. Then they tested whether giving them a stimulant like caffeine helps or doesn't help and whatnot. If they don't know how to use ESP to begin with how do they learn it? Normally, you try something, and you see whether it succeeds or fails, right?

Mishlove: Typically, that's how it's done.

Tart: If I think I'm going to touch the tip of my ear but instead I pat the top of my head, it doesn't feel very ear-ish up there and I get immediate feedback. This occurred to me as a very basic principle of learning anything, which had never been applied in ESP research.

Mishlove: The work that you did occurred when biofeedback was just coming to the forefront. There were some very significant studies that showed that people could learn how to control their heart rates and their brainwaves using feedback. That was a new finding back in the 1960s.

Tart: That was happening at the same time, and I saw the parallel there. If you give people feedback about something, there's a good chance they can learn to control it. So, I said to myself, okay, you must assume that a person has some potential ESP ability and if you put them in a learning situation instead of a testing situation maybe they can learn it. If they don't know how to do something like guessing through a whole deck of cards and then another deck, they undergo what in psychology is known as an extinction paradigm. You can take any skill a person has and, by making them do it over and over without feedback, they'll get worse and worse at it and gradually lose their skill altogether. That is one of the most solid repeatable findings in parapsychology: making people do these ESP tests over and over with no feedback causes them to get worse and worse.

Mishlove: It's known as the decline effect. It's often argued by skeptics that the decline effect proves there was never anything there to begin with.

Tart: It's a silly argument though because chance doesn't get tired. Chance runs along at the same variable level all the time. It's interesting as evidence that when people use ESP too much, they get tired and lose their talent. It's interesting in saying something about how it may work. But if your goal is to get ESP to happen regularly and reliably in the laboratory, it's a killer. I published this as a theory and it was not well received because one way of reading it is, "Hey, you folks who have sacrificed so much to do ESP tests in spite of the career drawbacks have been killing off the very phenomena you want to study."

Mishlove: You would think that would be useful information.

Tart: It is useful information, but it is not ego-syntonic, as I say.

Mishlove: Not welcome.

Tart: I don't like it when people point out that I'm being stupid. I try to remember that after I get over not liking it and that I should see if there's some truth there. Can I improve what I'm doing?

Mishlove: I do recall that it created a controversy in the field.

Tart: Having published it as a theory I said that theory is nice, I love it when stuff makes sense but there must be some data that supports it. I first did some rough and crude pilot studies, and I modified them in a very interesting way. I was teaching an upper-level undergraduate course on experimental psychology at the time using exercises on how to perform experiments. But I said, "No, let's do this like an apprenticeship situation where you're doing a real experiment that will actually teach us something with somebody who is supposedly an expert in it." As the instructor I'm defined as an expert. That made it much more interesting. So, after the first rough-and-ready experiment we did it in a much more formal way. First, we needed people who had some talent in ESP to begin with.

Mishlove: You had to pre-screen them.

Tart: I had roughly 20 students in the class, divide up into teams of two or three people. They would go and beg other instructors to give them the last ten minutes of one of their classes to do a mass ESP test with their students. Each class could vary from 15 or 20 students to several hundred. My students would pass out a response form then they did a little quick card guessing game.

Mishlove: That's amazing that you didn't lose your tenure right then and there.

Tart: It's hard to get tenure but it's harder to lose it fortunately. Some people would have done it if they could have but that is another story.

Mishlove: Now you're involving the whole psychology department in your research.

Tart: Actually, most of these were non-psychology classes. My students could go to any classes where they knew the instructor.

Mishlove: Because traditionally psychologists are the most hostile.

Tart: Yes. I'll tell you an interesting fact I found. J.B. Rhine (1895-1980) became famous for his ESP research after publishing his book which was very widely known to the public. He was working at the Duke University psychology department. As far as psychology and parapsychology went, I think he put Duke on the map. It was a good school, but it was relatively unknown before that. Then this famous ESP researcher …

Mishlove: He became virtually the most famous professor at Duke, and you were there.

Tart: Yes. But then when the other psychology department professors would attend conferences and people found out they were from Duke they said, "Oh, do you work with J.B. Rhine?" They hated it because they thought this ESP stuff was absolutely nuts. The interesting fact I learned was that someone had written to a secretary in the psychology department for a historical survey. They asked, "Do you ever get any letters for J.B. Rhine anymore, even though he's been dead for many years?" They said they get more letters for J.B. Rhine than for all the rest of the Duke University psychology faculty combined. So, his ghost is still making the psychologists embarrassed.

Psychologists are super defensive about ESP. One of my graduate school professors used to say that it was only a hundred years ago they let us out of the philosophy department and some of them would like to put us back because we're just using empty words. We want to be real scientists.

Mishlove: Compared to physicists they're at the bottom of the pecking order of scientists.

Tart: Exactly. Maybe economists are down there even lower. There was a lot of resistance in doing this kind of thing.

Mishlove: But you were able to get other professors, not psychologists, to help with this study.

Tart: Who knows how selective that was? Maybe it was due to the professors being bored teaching the same class repeatedly and they loved to have somebody taking the last 10 minutes. Anyway, my students screened roughly 2,000 candidates this way. We said that any individual who made a very high score on this would be considered possibly talented. Possibly, because when you test so many students some are going to score high by chance alone. If you take odds of 1 in 20 as significant then 1 out of 20 students is going to look significant by accident. We took the ones who seemed to be talented and brought them in for an individual test session using either of two machines where there was no problem with sensory leakage. By chance alone, the odds of someone scoring significantly on two consecutive tests if they have no ESP are very low. We said that anybody who continued to score high had potential talent, and we put them in the training study where we gave them feedback to see if they could learn.

Mishlove: You were a pioneer in the era of using automated machines for ESP testing.

Tart: I didn't start it, but I was one of the few active in those early days.

Mishlove: With your background in electronics, you designed the equipment, as I recall.

Tart: Yeah, I like machines.

Mishlove: But the point that I want to make is, this is what's known as a forced choice test.

Tart: Right.

Mishlove: It's not remote viewing.

Tart: No.

Mishlove: It was a 10-choice trainer as I recall.

Tart: There were two machines. One machine was a four-choice trainer. A ready light would come on, meaning somebody in the other room was trying to telepathically send the numbers 1-2-3 or 4, and you had to push a button that would indicate your guess. If you got it right a bell would ring, ding! A very nice bell so people got immediate feedback. If you were wrong, then the correct number light lit up. The other machine was a 10-choice trainer, so it was much harder to score well by chance. We then let people choose whether they want to continue the experiment on the 10-choice machine or the 4-choice machine. The 10-choice machine was the most exciting because it's harder to get a good score. We had five people who individually scored quite significantly, some of them with odds of millions to one against chance. None of them showed a decline effect even though declines were considered common. So, at the very least, by giving immediate feedback we weren't extinguishing ESP or confusing them. When they heard the bell ring if they felt a "cool certainty" about their choice they could keep exploring the "cool certainty" feeling rather than the tensed forehead or another behavior.

Mishlove: What you're talking about here are physiological cues that might be associated with correct ESP scores.

Tart: I used two physiological cues as an example, but they could be psychological ones too. You don't know whether the idea you have that it's number seven is ESP or not, but what else is happening? Do you feel especially relaxed? Do you feel sure? Do you hear a buzzing in your head? You can start sorting out that when certain kinds of experiences happen, that you're more likely to be right. When certain other kinds of experiences happen, you're almost always wrong and should not respond. They could also press a button to have that whole trial skipped.

Mishlove: The idea is that people will learn when to be confident and when not to be confident.

Tart: That's right. The results were very significant for ESP manifesting with no decline. It looked like they were starting to learn but it didn't go on long enough to give good learning opportunities. But it was a great start. Then one of the most interesting things that happened was a young woman who had done well on the 10-choice machine averaging 20 percent and on some of her runs she was hitting 30, 40, 50 percent started crying and would not go on with the experiment. If you're hitting a little bit above chance, the professor, says it is statistically significant, but you don't know. When you're hitting 40-50 percent on something that is that hard at the gut level you know *something* is going on. She was having to face up to the fact that she was psychic.

Mishlove: And that's frightening sometimes.

Tart: I heard from her many years later that she'd become a doctor. We had some other candidates who were very good at not hitting the correct button but pushed the button immediately to the other side of the correct button on the 10-choice machine. When they learned that we were scoring for that too they started hitting further and further away from the correct target because there can be resistance to being psychic. It's not that long in human history that we burned people at the stake who we thought were psychic.

Mishlove: A few hundred years ago.

Tart: In some cultures, it's been a lot less time.

Mishlove: In fact, I'd imagine if you scour the news reports you would see that even today it happens occasionally.

Tart: There is a level of fear of psychic abilities. We were trying to avoid that in this experiment. The greatest interest of mine and the main research project for all my life has been about my mind. Why do I do the things I do? Why do I tend to point to my head when I talk about my mind? How thoroughly have I been brainwashed to think that the brain is the seat of the mind? I notice for instance that in some ways I feared psychic abilities. If I denied my fear, then that could be a subconscious force that could affect experiments. When I admitted it to myself, I think it posed less of a problem. I can't prove it, but most parapsychologists will not admit to having any kind of fear of psi, which is one of the difficult problems.

This woman dropped out of the experiment because she passed that gut-level threshold that real stuff is happening here. I hope she became a good doctor. I think a good doctor sometimes makes psychic diagnoses and maybe she uses it without thinking it's psychic.

Mishlove: People are going to look back at your career as a parapsychologist thinking that one of the hallmarks is that you established, minimally speaking, that feedback can prevent the decline effect.

Tart: Yes, but then a strange thing happened. I thought that experimenters would start adopting the immediate feedback paradigm.

Hardly any parapsychologist did, and those who did ignored that you need people with some raw talent to begin with if you're going to train it. They used random people who didn't show any talent to begin with and the feedback didn't work which is a perfectly correct theoretical prediction but it's trivial. I think there was resistance and remote viewing came along, a new term for clairvoyance which had a much sexier experimental procedure, so I got diverted into that.

Mishlove: Remote viewing, or free response ESP, where people report on their mental imagery and then independent judges match that imagery against potential targets.

Tart: Good quick explanation which also says something interesting about the psychology involving ESP. If the target you're trying to guess is a number, between 1 and 10, part of you is going to try to game it. For instance, the reason ESP tests done with cards had no feedback until it was all over was that people would count the cards. If all the stars have been used up, I won't call stars anymore and I'll get a higher score which just shows that I have some functioning memory.

Mishlove: Also, with the ESP trainers the experiment is kinesthetic. You must reach out with your hand and push a button.

Tart: That was another interesting part of it too. This 10-choice trainer had a circle of lights about two feet in diameter with a switch by the side of each one. The middle light came on when someone was sending. We discovered—and eventually we put a TV camera in to watch this—that people would dowse around. What was even more interesting was often the signal light would come on that somebody was sending and the person receiving would immediately hover their hand over the correct target and then move away to push the wrong button. I would think, dammit, I need an electrical shock button for that. Their hand knew it but it didn't make it through to their conscious response processes.

Mishlove: Because the mind is always trying to work logically, which interferes with the ESP.

Tart: In fact, I did a further analysis that the more someone's style of responding was logical, as if they were playing the odds, the worse they did. You need to bring a completely open mind and forget what's happened before. It's totally irrelevant and is only going to distract you. People who were more open to the randomness got higher scores. It was very interesting stuff to learn about the psychology of psi. I think people can learn to use ESP better, or that everyone can, I don't know.

Mishlove: After you did this study, as I recall, or around the same time, you were hired to work at SRI, Stanford Research Institute, where they were developing the first remote viewing studies. You're a co-author of one of the important anthologies on remote viewing.

Tart: How much do you want to go into remote viewing?

Mishlove: Let's just talk about it in terms of the learning paradigm involving feedback.

Tart: Remote viewing incorporated almost immediate feedback routinely. I don't know whether it was deliberate or not. It might have been partially deliberate because Russell Targ and I had talked about feedback learning a great deal before they began the program. If you are doing a card guessing test, you're getting no immediate feedback. By the time you're guessing the 23rd card, you've got all sorts of memories of the other cards you guessed before.

Mishlove: The feedback on the forced choice must be trial by trial.

Tart: Which means you need to have an independent way of generating it each time, so card counting doesn't matter. But that is easily handled technically.

Mishlove: You can't give all the feedback at the end of 25 trials.

Tart: Let's say you got a hit on the 23rd card and when they finally turn over the deck and you look at it. Was that the one where you were trembling or was that the one where you felt uptight? There are so many things that you don't remember. With remote viewing, the usual procedure was that you did your viewing, and then they came back, and they drove you directly to the target for actual feedback without something confusing your memory of what you felt. It gives you an opportunity to say, "Okay, when I remote view this kind of thing, I'm generally accurate. With that kind of thing, I'm usually awfully relaxed about that." So immediate feedback came in there.

Mishlove: Remote viewers also might spend a whole afternoon on a single trial, whereas with your forced choice studies you're going to go through 20-30 trials in less than an hour.

Tart: If your model that this is a skill you need to learn, rushing people through it sounds like a very bad condition to learn anything. But giving them the leisure to introspect on what they're doing and what the consequences are decreases the hit rate.

Mishlove: I understand some remote viewers—I interviewed Joe McMoneagle, an outstanding remote viewer—seem to feel that it doesn't matter whether they get feedback.

Tart: Yeah, but Joe is outstanding. There are a few psychics who are good enough, even though they're not always right, that the conditions don't particularly matter. Some psychics need a supportive environment. Others love it when there's some pseudo skeptic there who says, "You're a bunch of crap. You're just faking it all." That's the challenge they need to motivate them. But those are individual foibles which are different from those of the usual run of remote viewers.

Mishlove: You're saying, overall, about remote viewing or free response ESP, feedback is still important.

Tart: Yes. I have not heard reports of decline effects in remote viewing. With immediate feedback they may be holding on to whatever level of talent they have initially. I don't know if there's been a consistent look at whether they learned to gradually get better or not. I think the research conditions, especially the ones focusing on operational remote viewing, didn't make it very easy to look at that.

Mishlove: As we were discussing before this interview there is a controversy around that question. But your experimental studies on feedback and learning to use ESP will stand, or in your mind at least, as one of your lasting contributions to the field.

Tart: It stands in my mind as my lasting contribution, though it has not been followed up on or it has been forgotten by most of the people in the field. It's a very interesting field we're involved with here.

Mishlove: Well, it's such a tiny field and my expectation is that in the future people will be very grateful to learn about the work that you did.

Tart: I hope so. Ordinarily in science, when you figure out how to do something better, colleagues want to come around and see how you do it. When lasers were first being developed, for instance, they had such low power, and it was speculation whether anybody could do anything with them. Russell Targ learned to build lasers that would drill a hole through a brick. A lot of people came to see how it was built. You would think that everybody would have run off to see what these remote viewing researchers were doing to get such good results. But we're kind of crazy. It's human nature.

Mishlove: There is an International Remote Viewing Association [IRVA] and there are hundreds of people following up, even though government research funding into remote viewing ended a long time ago. Charley Tart, thank you so much for sharing this important work with me.

Tart: Thank you for an opportunity to talk about it Jeffrey. I hope it turns out to be useful for somebody.

Mishlove: I think it will.

7

Remote Viewing Psychology

～

Recorded on November 9, 2016

Jeffrey Mishlove: Hello and welcome. I'm Jeffrey Mishlove. Today, we'll be exploring the psychology of remote viewing. With me is Professor Charles Tart, an emeritus professor of psychology at the University of California, Davis, and an emeritus professor at the Institute of Transpersonal Psychology. Professor Tart was my mentor and a faculty member on my doctoral dissertation committee when I was a graduate student in parapsychology at Berkeley. He is the author of numerous books in the field and over 100 scientific papers in parapsychology. His publications include the classic anthology, *Altered States of Consciousness*. His other books include *Learning to Use Extrasensory Perception* and *Psi: Scientific Studies of the Psychic Realm*. He is also a co-editor of an important anthology on remote viewing called *Mind at Large*, which he co-edited with Russell Targ and Hal Puthoff when he was an associate at SRI International, or the Stanford Research Institute when it was doing pioneering work in remote viewing. Welcome, Charley.

Charles Tart: It's good to be here, Jeff.

Mishlove: It's a pleasure to be with you. You were there to witness, or very close to witnessing, the birth of the discipline of remote viewing.

Tart: Yeah, those were interesting times in the late 1970s, if I have my chronology right. Several people in the Bay area were interested in parapsychological research. I've known Russell Targ for a zillion years, and he and Hal gave a presentation on their remote viewing experiments and gave several examples. I was very interested because the quality and intensity of the ESP seemed to be a lot higher than we got using the usual multiple-choice guessing tests.

After they gave several good examples of remote viewings, they said, "Okay, we're going to demonstrate it to you. Hal is going to leave, and in half an hour, he'll be somewhere that he can drive to," which narrows it down to about two million targets in the Bay Area. Hal left, and about half an hour later, Russell told us to use some paper and a pencil to write down any visual images of where Hal might be. I drew something, but I didn't expect to see anything because I don't think of myself as psychic. We wrote down our impressions for 15 minutes, and after another 15 minutes or so later, Hal came back. Russell said, "Good, we'll take you to the target now."

I had made a little rough drawing of what I thought was some kind of factory. There were white machines with a lot of circular motion in them, and the whole factory was lit very brightly. Hal and Russell took us someplace on University Avenue, where we parked and walked over. We stopped in front of this store, but nothing looked anything like what I had remote-viewed until I stepped over three feet further and looked through the window of a laundromat and saw all the white washers and dryers spinning loads in a very bright place. I said, "Oh, they got some remote viewing out of me. That's impressive."

Mishlove: Was that the target?

Tart: That was the target. I was just standing in the wrong place. Hal had stood there right in front of the window, looking into the laundromat. It's a wonder he wasn't arrested for loitering like that. That was a personal introduction for me that this remote viewing can get interesting.

Mishlove: Because in your decades as a parapsychologist, you weren't particularly an experiencer.

Tart: No, I never thought of myself as an experiencer. When people ask me how I got interested in parapsychology, they're always hoping for a good story. God dropped by one day and said, "Young man, thou shalt do parapsychology."

Mishlove: I have stories like that.

Tart: For me, it was much more an intellectual thing, reading literature to deal with my conflict between science and religion.

Mishlove: But your experience, as I understand it, is quite typical of the accomplished, self-confident professional people who Hal and Russell worked with when given a new, supposedly impossible task.

Tart: Yes. That's one of the most important things about the psychology of remote viewing. Most parapsychology and psychology experiments use college sophomores as subjects. Some witty person once defined psychology as the study of college sophomores by former college sophomores for the benefit of future college sophomores. Well, college sophomores are unclear about a lot of things. However, the people that they used as remote viewers at SRI were almost always contract monitors, visiting government officials, and the like. As you say, they were people used to doing difficult things that were shown that other people like them were successful, so they did it. They didn't think of themselves as psychic, but they were used to succeeding at what they were doing.

Mishlove: We ought to point out that that research was funded by the government for 20 years.

Tart: Oh, yes.

Mishlove: One reason, I think, is that the contract monitors who came in from Washington, DC, were asked to remote view, and it's very hard for them to say this is all bunko when they're successful.

Tart: The monitors come in and say, "I'm skeptical. Show me an example of remote viewing." Hal and Russell would say, "Sure, and you're the viewer." That tended to catch people off guard.

Mishlove: It also created a distinction between remote viewers and people who think of themselves as psychics. Remote viewers often say, "I'm not psychic, but I can do remote viewing."

Tart: Interesting distinction.

Mishlove: By this, they mean they don't burn candles, read tarot cards, or do past-life readings, and so on.

Tart: But that's the first big clue about the psychology of successful remote viewing: work with successful people, not people unsure of who they are and what they want to do in life. I was impressed enough that I thought about taking a year off from teaching at Davis to work on the project with them. My department was initially a little hostile about my leave of absence, but on the other hand, some of them were probably glad to get this weirdo who does ESP studies away for a year. I managed to get some leave, and I went down and worked as a consultant.

The next big clue about the project's importance came when I first arrived there. There was a guard at the entrance. This was a secure facility, not some college campus with kids in t-shirts wandering around. This was a big deal. I couldn't go right in unless one of the investigators fetched me and guided me around for the rest of the day. I had to sign in and get a temporary badge. I was undergoing a major psychological procedure already.

Mishlove: It's a big military-industrial think tank.

Tart: This is a big important place, and I was being treated in a special way. It seemed even more dangerous in a way because of the security all over the place. Then the next amazing thing was—I forget whether it was Hal or Russ who escorted me—they took me up to their lab, which was in another building, but rather than just traveling along the corridors, they took shortcuts through a few other labs. These labs were full of the most fascinating scientific equipment, the computers computing, the lights blinking. It was very clear to me that I was in the temple of big science. When they finally got me to their lab, they showed me examples of how one of the contract monitors viewed things. By then, my mind was blown, and I realized this is what happens to all the people who come here: they get indoctrinated. This is not what some low-paid professor doing a project with college sophomores has. This is a big deal. That makes an enormous difference. They also didn't do a whole bunch of experiments one day but focused on an individual for at least half a day to prepare them for a remote viewing.

Mishlove: A single trial.

Tart: Yeah. A single trial and you get feedback on how well you did which was so different.

Mishlove: Test subjects were not treated like college students at all, and Hal Puthoff and Russell Targ have one of the best track records in all of parapsychology.

Tart: During that year that I was at SRI, the feeling that pervaded all the experiments was, "We didn't get any psychic stuff in this experiment. What did we do wrong?" Instead of, "Gee, we were lucky this year. We got two experiments that worked." They had a well-earned confidence that things would work.

Here's a funny observation. I was talking to Russell once after he'd been doing Remote Viewing experiments for several years. He said, "Every once in a while, I begin to think that there can't be psychic stuff. It's like the social conditioning increases and I need to see a good remote viewing to remind me, oh yeah, this stuff works." When you're exposed to it all the time, it totally shifts your view of what's possible in the world.

Mishlove: What was your role you had during the year you were there?

Tart: I played several different roles. One was very interesting where I tried to understand the judging process. A viewer remote views a place and then a formal evaluation of their transcript is mixed in with a bunch of other transcripts describing other places. A judge compares each transcript to the target location. The judge is blinded so they don't know what transcript goes with what target. If there is nothing but chance operating or just vague generalities, then we know by chance there will just be a few matches.

But, if they're getting things correctly by remote viewing, there will be a lot more matches than you get by chance, and it can be evaluated statistically. You solve the problem of a judge being too credulous or super skeptical so, I worked on the psychology of that. It turned out judging was very complicated.

Mishlove: The judging is just as important as the viewing.

Tart: I thought I was going to understand the major dimensions of judging and figure out how to make it more efficient quickly. But having acted as a judge a few times and analyzing other judges, it was more difficult than I had expected. If somebody says, "I see a tall, red building," is that a single object that's present or absent? Does any tall object or any red object count as a hit? How far should you break things down? It gets tricky. If you have a tremendously accurate remote viewing, it is easily judged. But when it's more marginal, it's hard to break that down.

Furthermore, the judging has one great disadvantage. It doesn't give you a precise measure of just how much psi is involved in the remote viewing. If you give me a pool of ten targets and all I do is give you the correct name of the street each target is on, there will be a perfect matching. But if that is the only information I gave you, it doesn't sound like much psi at all, even though it happened to be a crucial hit.

Mishlove: A street name is good.

Tart: How do you estimate how much information is at a target location? Because that's one of the things that would help us understand what the psychic process is.

Mishlove: Information rates.

Tart: Yeah, what's the information rate?

Mishlove: Where do you begin to match it with communication theory, for example.

Tart: That turned out to be very hard. We held a mini conference once with several judges to find out what kind of techniques they used with thoughts of publishing a manual. But I don't think we ever got clear enough input for it to be worthwhile.

Mishlove: A manual would be useful. A *Newsweek* story published in November 2015 was about Ed May, who ran the program for ten years after it left SRI and received government funding. One of the criticisms mentioned in the article was that it only worked so well because Ed May himself did all the judging.

Tart: You could just have a psychic judge. The remote viewing could have been lousy, but the judge is psychic enough to match up the transcript with the location. So, what do you do? Tell the judge to not be psychic? If you could make the judging something purely logical, such as using a checklist: Is there something red: yes, or no? Is there something tall: yes, or no? You could minimize psychic interference, but otherwise a psychic judge might be a real contaminating factor.

Mishlove: There are judging protocols that are like the ones you described, where they might have 20 or 30 qualitative items. I don't know if that protocol works so well.

Tart: It's got advantages and disadvantages because the way the checklist is put together is an item of information. If you've disassembled this tall red building into something tall, something red, or some kind of building, you may miss another crucial aspect of the remote viewing. So, it's not like we know the best way to judge it. There's a lot that could be developed there.

Mishlove: I want to clarify one point regarding Ed May. Even though he was apparently the only judge for a long time, Ed's counter to the critic Ray Hyman was that he used double blinding.

Tart: If your judge is double-blind, that's all that matters because the judge should not know what reading was intended for what target. That was one of the first things I did with my consulting work at SRI. Their original reports had been published in *Nature* which garnered a scathing attack by a couple of Australian psychologists, Marks and Kammann. They said that when judges looked at the transcripts, they could see, for instance, a reference to a viewing done the previous day. Given that sequence, the judge could logically match things up. I reanalyzed those issues pulling out all the statements that would give judges clues.

Mishlove: You removed those statements and then had it rejudged.

Tart: After I worked on those statements, the judge might match two or three of the things rather than eight of the nine or something like that. I also brought in a new judge who used the updated statements, and he matched things just as well as the previous judges had. However, it was a reasonable criticism. They hadn't learned the importance of getting rid of supposedly irrelevant stuff, but if you want to push the guessing hypothesis further, it matters.

Mishlove: So, because you were part of the research team, you were necessarily very sensitive to criticisms that had been in the literature from skeptical investigators.

Tart: I had been sensitive to that for a long time before that because I've been reading the work of the pseudo skeptics since I was a teenager.

Mishlove: Do you consider all the skeptics pseudo skeptics?

Tart: I try to never use words like *all*, but let's say at least 95 percent. A skeptic is someone who says, "The current explanation of why such and such happens strikes me as inadequate. I'd like to find a better explanation that fits the facts better." A skeptic is open-minded and curious, and they want to know. The pseudo skeptics are people who say, "I believe what they reported couldn't have happened, and I want the prestige of appearing to be scientific and logical, so I'm going to call myself a skeptic," but they're debunkers. By and large, I have no respect for the pseudo skeptics. They are proponents of an alternate worldview who want to appear scientific but break all the rules of logic and scientific method to attack things.

Mishlove: But in the case of Marks and Kammann that you just mentioned, they, through their criticism, helped you to tighten the protocol a bit, and so that can be useful.

Tart: That one turned out to be useful. But the most helpful skeptics, who recommend changes, almost always come from within parapsychology itself. I've criticized some experiments, and the experimenter realized they had to do better.

Mishlove: I'm aware that parapsychologists can be extremely critical of each other. Sometimes, to a fault.

Tart: Yes, sometimes to a fault. There's this issue of resistance to and fear of psychic functioning even among people who are supposed to be objective scientists. But who wants to say that they're afraid? "Hey, I'm a big, tough scientist. I'm not afraid of anything, but my reasonable criticisms of this show there's a flaw." One of the ways this comes out is in a phenomenon I've called the religion of the 0.05 P value. What do I mean by that? If you do an experiment, say, with card guessing, and instead of getting 20% right, which would be what chance would predict, somebody averages 22% over a long period which is statistically significant at the 0.05 P value. The occurrence of less than five in a hundred times is the customary level for assuming that something is happening.

If you present a paper at the Parapsychological Association meeting and it's significant at the 0.05 level, there won't be any criticisms of it unless there is a major methodological fault. It's unlikely that papers with a flaw would make it through the selection committee. If you do an experiment where the psychic effect is much stronger than that, all sorts of methodological criticisms come up that I suspect are driven by a fear of psi. If it's a little statistical effect, we do not consider the implications of it.

Take psychokinesis, for instance, the ability of the mind to affect matter. If you get a little bit more than one-sixth of a particular side using a machine for rolling dice, that's interesting in an abstract sort of way. But if somebody could regularly produce one ounce of push by psychic means for a minute, they could kill anybody they want to just by closing the mitral valve in the heart and depriving the brain of blood. It would be a completely undetectable crime because the victim had heart failure. It's not been that long since people burned psychics at the stake.

Mishlove: There is some discussion in the anthropology literature about what they call death by hexing. There are some documented cases that suggest this is a real possibility.

Tart: Although, of course, anthropologists have a lot of trouble with this possibility. An anthropologist friend once told me a very amusing story about when he was with some shamans of a South American tribe, and they'd been talking about people who'd been killed by magic. Western science explains that when the person knows they're cursed, since they've been culturally conditioned to believe in curses, the anxiety produces physiological effects causing death.

Mishlove: The stress response kicks in, but there are cases where they didn't even know it.

Tart: But when he told the shamans this, they all rolled on the floor laughing. "That's what you Westerners believe? You get a shaman to protect you if you know you've been hexed. The only effective hexes are ones you don't know about. You Westerners are something." Now, as far as I know, there are no parapsychological experiments being done on nasty uses of psi like that which is fine with me. I don't want it to be possible, but I wouldn't say it's *not* possible.

Mishlove: We could look at some of the studies that were done in the old Soviet Union. I think they did look at some of those things.

Tart: They did some of them there, but the ones I've looked at so far were wild. They weren't being very scientific.

Mishlove: Since you brought up shamanism, I understand that in the shamanistic training literature there's a great deal we could learn about remote viewing. To become a shaman, it's often a requirement to be sent off into the jungle to find objects that have been hidden.

Tart: A person is often picked to be trained as a shaman because something strange is happening with them. When a kid in our culture has something strange happen to them, what do we do? We send them to the doctor because they must be sick and may be given drugs to suppress whatever is happening. That is not a supportive environment like being told that you may have the talent to become a shaman and be apprenticed with that good shaman in the next village. What a difference that can make.

One of my students at the Institute of Transpersonal Psychology did his dissertation research on what he called the "bright shadow". This was a term I had never heard before, although it's a term he said that Carl Jung had used. Most people have heard of the shadow part of our minds: the shameful parts that we repress and don't want to own up to. But it turns out there has always been a fair number of kids who have some fantastic spiritual experience, just like a grown-up might have. However, when they tell someone about it, they're told the devil's possessing them, or they're sick and need to be taken to the doctor, and they end up repressing this part of themselves to get by. Later in life, they realize they took a vital part of their psyche and squeezed it down making their life lacking because of that.

This happened to my student, which created a considerable personal interest. If they can do psychological work to un-repress this bright shadow part, it would be very important. So, you have someone that may be psychic, and in one culture you're told you're nuts and need to be institutionalized because you must be schizophrenic. Some of the old tests of psychopathology included a belief in psychic stuff.

Mishlove: By definition.

Tart: By definition. Instead, if you're told you're talented, it's very different.

Mishlove: Charley, this has been a wonderful discussion.

Tart: Just remember, Jeff, you're probably talented rather than crazy. All the audience, too. Now, let me add that you can be crazy, but that's independent of whether you're psychic.

Mishlove: You might be both.

Tart: Right. You might be both. But just because you've had an unusual psychic or spiritual experience does not automatically mean you're mentally ill in any form.

Mishlove: Thank you for being with me, Charley.

Tart: My pleasure.

8

Fear of Psi

~

Recorded on November 9, 2016

Mishlove: Hello and welcome. I am Jeffrey Mishlove. Today we'll be exploring the fear of psychic power or psychic functioning. Psi, as parapsychologists call it. My guest, Charles Tart, is Emeritus Professor at the University of California Davis and the Institute of Transpersonal Psychology.

Welcome again, Charley.

Tart: Good to be here, Jeff.

Mishlove: It's a pleasure to be with you, truly.

Tart: I don't know how much of a pleasure it will be to talk about the fear of psi. I hate fear myself, but we shall see.

Mishlove: The interesting thing about fear of psi is many people, even in the parapsychology community, are in denial there is such a thing as fear of psi. Yet we live in a culture where people, even a few hundred years ago, were burnt at the stake for their ostensible psychic powers.

Tart: It is funny if you think about it. Historically, humanity has always believed that some people have malevolent psychic abilities. If you could hire them to work on your side, that may be socially acceptable. But the very idea of having them out there, created hysterical mob

95

reactions occasionally. Then some old lady gets burned because she looks funny. And yet somehow, we are now in a rational stage. Society today considers such thoughts as crazy and nonsensical.

Mishlove: One of my former mentors, you probably remember him, Arthur M. Young (1905-1995), used to remark that the archetype, for the epitome of a paradigm shift, is witchcraft. In one era we say, "Witches must be burnt at the stake." And the next era we say, "Oh, witchcraft doesn't exist."

Tart: That's quite a shift, and of course it is not uniform. I think the reality is there is still a lot of fear. Most of which is dealt with by never thinking about it: a common human way of handling problems.

Mishlove: I know as a parapsychologist, and I'm sure you've had this same experience. I think every lecturer in parapsychology has an acquaintance with this moment. We give a lecture, and somebody comes up afterwards, and then preface their remarks by saying, "I have never told this to anyone before."

Tart: I've heard that line.

Mishlove: "I have never told this to anyone. But let me tell you; I need to talk to somebody."

Tart: The most interesting versions have been from people, many who are scientists, sometimes prominent scientists. They would never mention a psi experience to any of their scientist colleagues. They would be considered crazy or becoming senile or something like that. That's why I started this website, *The Archives of Scientists' Transcendent Experiences* (TASTE). It gave them a place to express psychic and spiritual experiences out of the ordinary. And this turned out to be a very interesting project because I figured, okay, a lot of these people need to get it off their chest, somehow. They're sensible enough to realize it is not socially acceptable. I set up the website so people who were scientists could write to me. Then I would know who they were, but they could post their experience anonymously.

While I ran the website—I closed it down eventually for lack of time to keep it up—but while I ran it, about half of them chose to be anonymous. The other half did not. But it was interesting, the ones who were okay with using their real names were almost completely retired scientists. They did not have to worry anymore about what their colleagues thought of them. The taboo against just thinking something psychic happened can be very strong.

Mishlove: And very real. Scientists may lose prestige, sometimes their positions, often their funding, simply for being publicly associated with parapsychology.

Tart: We know the example, for instance, of Nobel Prize winner Brian Josephson. He expressed an interest in parapsychological things and was uninvited to academic conferences, where he was slated the star speaker. Only because of his association with the paranormal. Really, this is weird, unscientific behavior.

Mishlove: The social stigma around parapsychology is not so different from those associated with sexual deviancy or racial bias or other social prejudice. In fact, I think most of the others are being addressed now. We see the legalization of gay marriage, for example. Parapsychology has not yet achieved the social leverage to have a large-scale address of that fear.

Tart: I used to commute to work in a carpool with a lot of women faculty members. They were very much into feminism and its politics. I used to tease them sometimes with comments like, I'm a member of a minority that is unfairly persecuted, too. But we are such a small minority in parapsychology that we don't have any leverage.

Mishlove: The fear of being persecuted is a real fear. Fear of going insane or being insane or being thought of as insane, well, that might be real. I don't know of many people who have gone insane because they took an interest in parapsychology.

Tart: Where would we find any statistics on it? I do know a lot of those admitting to having psychic and spiritual experiences were treated badly. They were referred to psychiatrists, some committed to mental institutions. All justified because of an unusual psi experience; it must be a sign of craziness. I have ended up as a therapist to some, even though it wasn't part of my life's career plan. I started training in clinical psychology in graduate school because I thought it would be hard to make a living from my interests alone. There was plenty of need for therapists. But I gave it up after a while. I did not possess enough emotional intelligence, was my thinking then. And I knew the tests and meds available then weren't good.

But I've had hundreds of phone calls and letters and the like over the years. All from people admitting what to me is a garden variety psychic experience. They worried they were going crazy. The fact that

I, as a professor, as something of an authority figure, can tell them, no, no, no. This experience doesn't necessarily mean you are going crazy. This is the kind of thing that happens to most people, except they never talk about it. So, they think it's weird and worry about it. It has a name like telepathy or clairvoyance, and it does not mean you're necessarily going crazy. You should still be discreet about who you talk to about it. There are a lot of prejudiced people out there who get excited about psi. Most of my callers have been greatly relieved by five minutes of conversation. A few, I think, were crazy. I mean, they needed some mental health support. Whether you're mentally ill or mentally normal has nothing to do with whether you have psychic experiences. They happen to everybody.

Mishlove: I do believe there is some research suggesting that people reporting spontaneous psychic experiences also report a greater incidence of early childhood abuse.

Tart: That certainly has been the case for some people who have turned out to be quite psychic later in life. I'm thinking of Eileen Garrett, for instance. She had an extremely lonely and persecuted kind of childhood. The only people she could play with were her so-called imaginary playmates. This occurs with a lot of people.

Mishlove: So there may be a relationship. Imaginary playmates may be a kind of doorway into the psychic realm.

Tart: Some people are lucky enough to take these unusual things and use them as an opening or as a growth challenge. But some people just suffer because they are told it's crazy.

Mishlove: There are a couple of interesting directions we could take here. I think it's worth mentioning, since you brought up the name of Eileen Garrett, that she is considered one of the great mediums and psychics of an earlier era. She's the founder of the Parapsychology Foundation. You knew her personally.

Tart: Oh, yes. When I went to college—I went to MIT—I was going to be an engineer, and that put me in Boston. There was the Exeter Street Theater nearby that showed a lot of foreign films. Considered far out in its day. It was owned by a couple of lady spiritualists. They brought other spiritualists and parapsychologists, esoteric teachers and the like, in to give lectures. I started attending and one of them was Eileen Garrett. I'm the kind of student that lecturers love. I have questions and ask interesting things. So, soon I was being invited back to tea afterwards with the speakers and met Mrs. Garrett that way. She was something; I'd never known anybody else like her.

Mishlove: She did a lot to promote the acceptance of psychic functioning through her foundation.

Tart: I don't know. She certainly helped a lot of researchers by giving out small grants so they could get started on research. She gave me my first grant to do some research in parapsychology. I was using hypnosis to see if people could have an out-of-the-body experience. It was amazing. She gave me a $100 grant, a fortune to me back then. I could then buy a tape recorder and stuff. At the end of the grant, I was writing up the report and I told her I had something like $5.50 left over. Should I send it back? And she said, no, keep the change. Grants aren't like that anymore.

Mishlove: It's interesting that a lot of early parapsychology research was funded by a psychic woman.

Tart: Yes. She was also a very successful businesswoman. Possibly one of the early feminists and making it quite clear women could do just fine.

Mishlove: And a publishing company.

Tart: And her foundation still exists. I've known her daughter and her granddaughter. Her granddaughter, Lisette Coly, still runs the foundation. I was just talking with her recently. We discussed how important it is to have an organization with continuity over the years. It doesn't have much money to donate, but small grants, here and there, can be the powerful triggers to launch a research career.

Mishlove: Another look at the fear of psi is its influence, not just on the researchers and those having psychic experiences, but the skeptics as well; the irrational scoffers.

Tart: The pseudo skeptics. Yes. As I've said before, I like the idea of skeptics. Skepticism is an honorable role. It means you're looking at the current explanation of something and you don't think it is very good. You're curious. You would like to see a better explanation. So, you want to help search for the truth. Skeptics now, in almost all cases, are not interested in helping to look for truth. They already know the truth: parapsychological stuff cannot possibly happen. They attack the research. It's like they are defending a religious orthodoxy against heresy. As if trying to pretend they are scientific and rational. I'm very disappointed in the skeptics. I'm a skeptic in the sense that I don't think our explanations about most things are very good. I'm all for finding other ones. This means I must take a chance that the ideas I know the truth about are wrong.

Mishlove: It seems to me it's reasonable for a psychologist to begin to question the motives of skeptics, not their conscious motives but unconscious.

Tart: Yes. I'd like to do that because many of these pseudo skeptics are highly intelligent people. Many are scientists in some other area of science. They don't follow the rules of science. If I think somebody's research is coming to the wrong conclusions, I try to see how the research could be improved. I do not contact funding agencies to stop financial support for them. Nor do I attack them.

One of the primary examples occurred when I was very new in this field. There was an article in *Science*. Now, *Science* was, and still is, one of the most prestigious scientific journals in the world. If you publish something in there, it's a big deal. There was an article on "Science and the Supernatural" by a chemist. His basic conclusion was that no intelligent person can read the evidence for extrasensory perception and doubt that it exists.

Mishlove: Price was his name as I recall.

Tart: Yes, George Price. *But*, since we know it is impossible, we must conclude all this evidence is due to error and fraud. Whoa, that's religious dogmatism. That's not science. What in the world was that doing in there? But this was an attitude very commonplace then. And still too commonplace.

Mishlove: It's still common and on the internet. It is like there are armies of trolls. They often post comments on the NTA interviews. I keep them if they are polite, but often they're very rude. I usually delete those.

Tart: When someone first told me a biographical note was published about me on Wikipedia, I thought, oh? So, naturally I looked it up. It was all right. It had been copied from something I'd posted. Occasionally I checked on it. I noticed my bio kept changing. Innocent things that happened in my career now took on a sinister meaning. I taught at the University of Nevada for a year as a distinguished visiting professor.

They wanted me to stay on. But no, I had other commitments. This was then described in my Wiki bio as if I'd been asked to leave. Just little things like that. From a Machiavellian point of view, some of the pseudo skeptics are very good at pushing their case. They are debaters for whom winning is the only thing, not the truth.

Mishlove: A foremost skeptic, the late Martin Gardner, wrote an autobiographical account of his life. In it he pointed out that he was raised in a fundamentalist Christian family. He learned to fear the devil; be afraid of the devil. Then he became enlightened and realized that what he needed to fear was, what he named, the rising tide of superstition. He transferred all that fear of the devil to now, fearing the rising tide of superstition. It was not very different.

Tart: When Gardner first began that change, psychology did not yet have much of an idea about emotional intelligence. Thank God we're starting to get it now. A person can be quite brilliant intellectually, but emotions may take over and distort things. Gurdjieff talked about how the emotional brain is faster than the intellectual brain. Today we know the neurology of it. Sensory signals to your senses come in and go through several neural relays, before they get to your consciousness. Each one takes a little bit of time. But the path splits into two junctions very quickly. The shorter path goes to the old emotional brain. So, the old emotional brain might pick up on a situation before the intellect even knows something is happening. Then say, uh-oh, scary, threatening, red alert. By the time the intellectual brain starts getting the message, you're already all up tight and ready to run or fight. Your rational mind becomes distorted.

Mishlove: You are saying something very important here, about the human condition, not just about psi and parapsychology. We are very emotional creatures.

Tart: And it turns out that talking about the emotional brain being faster is one of the most useful things I've ever taught to students. When we're too emotional, we tend to blame ourselves: why can't I control it, how can I be calmer? Once you discover we are hardwired to be faster with an emotional response, that gives you more of an opportunity to say, okay, the more primitive part of my brain caught me up. Let me try and relax instead of lashing out. I can give this situation a little more conscious intellectual thought. Not that emotion should be suppressed, but we've got to have a balance between intellect, emotion, body intelligence, as the emotional brain just is. Its philosophy was expressed in the old westerns: shoot first and ask questions later.

Mishlove: That's a good way to put it.

Tart: And it's laughable, but it creates an awful lot of useless suffering. Suffering that may have been avoided if somebody had paused a couple of seconds to think.

Mishlove: About parapsychology, we have a situation today where large numbers of people are afraid of psi for religious reasons. Psychic phenomena are real, they believe. But it's all the work of the devil and must be avoided. Then there are others thinking of the inverse. They believe that psychic phenomena does not exist, but we must be afraid of the rising tide of superstition. This tiny, little niche population—one or two percent and in the middle—often say, let's look at it scientifically. Let us discover the outcomes of scientific research.

Tart: Unfortunately, I think it's smaller than one or two percent. You're sitting with a foremost exponent of it here. I don't have many people I can talk to about this subject. I have spoken to some religious people, and in some ways, they are the harsher rejectionists. These are the people who state that, scientifically, they are rejecting psychic phenomena, because they already know the truth from their religion. To question becomes some kind of heresy, that must be defended.

Mishlove: I do think, Charley, from my perspective, in producing this video series—we have hundreds of thousands of views on these videos—that there is a growing segment, you could name them cultural creatives or a rebirth of a kind of secular spirituality or Gnosticism, that this segment of the population is growing.

Tart: And I plead with them to make me a liar for that last statement. We can be rational about this. I think it's possible to be faced with a situation and say, well, my spiritual beliefs' voice, it must be like so and so. I realize I'm very attached to those beliefs. My motivation for being attached to them is good. But am I that smart? Am I so smart that I cannot look more closely at what is going on and consider other possibilities? I can envision a kind of experimental spirituality someday. One where we say, yeah, important things are happening. Let's explore the range of what has happened. Let's explore the consequences. Dogmatic fundamentalism has a lot of consequences that are extremely negative. Open-minded spirituality can have a lot of positive consequences, as well as being so wishy-washy that it doesn't mean anything. There is a balance to be learned. It's between spiritual principles you want to stick to but be open to learning.

Mishlove: I think, though, there are deeper issues. We often speak of irrational fears, but there is a psychological dynamic. As somebody opens to psychic functioning, questions may emerge such as, is my ego going to disappear? Will I vanish myself as a ...

Tart: While other spiritual traditions talk about how incredibly hard it is to make the ego vanish.

Mishlove: They do, but there is fear associated with it.

Tart: Yeah. So, let me drop this to a deeper level and speak about where I'm coming from on this subject. In a conventional sense, I am primarily a scientific person. On the inside, I think of myself primarily as a spiritual seeker. That doesn't mean I know all sorts of absolute truths. I basically work from the premise that there is an intelligence in the universe. I usually don't call it God because that gets things too excited. But we don't have any other good words for it. There's an intelligence, a compassion, and so forth. My childhood told me we are made in God's image. God is intelligent. So, when we use our intelligence, we are actually praising God. But I also understand that we are talking about very powerful stuff that some people experience. It's not just gentle, gentle, there, there, everything is fine, it's all right. Rather, the experiences can be immense.

Mishlove: It could be much more than a little synchronicity here and there.

Tart: There is a legitimate concern that it may be too much. We must deal with that somehow. We must separate it from the irrational fears that somebody else is going to hex me or similar. But if we squash the whole subject down, trying to make it go away—that doesn't work.

Mishlove: You spoke about an exercise you sometimes give to your students. "I have a pill here ..." Let's conclude with that story.

Tart: I gave a lecture once for the American Society for Psychical Research in New York City. A big turnout—and afterwards they had a reception for me at headquarters. There were many parapsychologists attending, some who devoted their careers to studying ESP at great cost to themselves. I mentioned in a little off-the-cuff talk afterwards that sometimes I thought I was afraid of psychic phenomena. It gets weird, and I asked, did anyone else have this problem? Nobody had so, I thought, "well, maybe I'm kind of neurotic." But out of 30 or 40 people here in this room, I said, " ... no, come on."

Yet nobody raised their hand. I quickly devised this exercise, a little belief experiment. I have a pill in my pocket. I'm from California, okay. If you take this pill, you will become telepathic. You will know the thoughts and feelings of anybody within 100 yards of you. You will only have to take the pill once because it's a permanent change. Now, how many here want this pill? Nobody said anything. I said, how many want the pill? This philosophical discussion broke out about very abstract things. I said, "no, how many want the pill?" Finally, I shouted, "*how many want the pill?*" Nobody wants the pill. This is very interesting compared to the abstract philosophy. There is hesitancy and fear about becoming truly psychic. I've since done this test in more systematic ways with various groups. I have them write down their reasons. Would I be responsible, if I found someone was suicidal? Would I be driven nuts by the thoughts of all these people? Maybe there are good reasons we are generally not psychic.

Mishlove: It seems as if the nervous system itself is a filter. It keeps things out, largely. We all protect ourselves against the pain of the world. The suffering of others. It can be overwhelming. Usually, we let just enough in to be manageable.

Tart: The other day my daughter was over, and she started talking about this horrible world event. After a minute I told her, I don't want to talk about this. It makes me depressed. There is nothing I can do about it, so let's not talk about it. She kept right on talking. I asked again, could we not? She kept right on talking. So, I said, okay, I'm going to go in the other room and do something else. I walked out calmly. My wife and daughter thought I was horrible. I explained again, it's pain I cannot do anything about. It will just make me depressed. Your story will not make me capable of doing anything more helpful, but by not buying it—Oh, it's complicated. I don't have answers, but we must look at the problem more if we hope to find answers.

Mishlove: Charley Tart, thank you for sharing this discussion with me. I think the fear of psi is a very important issue.

Tart: Yeah, too important.

Mishlove: Thank you for being with me.

Tart: Thank you for the opportunity of this discussion, Jeff.

Mishlove: And (to the audience) thank you for being with us.

Tart: And remember to make a liar out of me.

9

Psychological Reflections on G. I. Gurdjieff

~

Recorded on November 9, 2016

Jeffrey Mishlove (JM): Hello and welcome. I'm Jeffrey Mishlove. Today we'll be sharing some psychological reflections on the teachings of the early 20th century mystic George Ivanovich Gurdjieff (1866-1949). Professor Charles Tart, an emeritus professor of psychology at the University of California, Davis, and the Institute for Transpersonal Psychology is with me today. Dr. Tart is an old friend and mentor. He is the author of many important books in the field of psychology, including *Waking Up*, a book largely based on the teachings of Gurdjieff. Some of Dr. Tart's other titles include *States of Consciousness; Open Mind, Discriminating Mind*; and the classic anthology *Altered States of Consciousness*. Welcome, Charley.

Charles Tart: Hi, Jeff.

Mishlove: Pleasure to be with you. Let's talk a little bit about who Gurdjieff was. I imagine many of our viewers have never heard nor read about him.

Tart: He was born in what today we call Armenia, unless the politics have changed since the last time I looked on a globe. He grew up as a nominal Christian, but in a very multicultural area. It was in one of those areas, conquered by a variety of empires every 50 or 100 years, that was instrumental in a constant mix of the population. Gurdjieff was exposed to many different religious traditions there. And this is where he gradually developed the conviction that religious tradition possessed some genuine knowledge, inherited in a purer form, from some time ago. But he reasoned, they polluted the information through various religious activities. He got very, very interested: could he find the source of this information? Was this real spiritual knowledge still available anywhere? Gurdjieff spent much of his life searching. And he believed he found a major source. Maybe *the* major source, then began teaching it until he died in the 1940s.

Mishlove: So, he was a seeker for much of his life.

Tart: Yes, very much a seeker.

Mishlove: Then he became a teacher. Probably some viewers are aware of the Peter Brook movie based on his book, *Meetings with Remarkable Men.*

Tart: Fantastic movie.

Mishlove: Yes, a very worthwhile movie.

Tart: Particularly this scene toward the end where the monks are performing sacred dances. Gurdjieff taught these to his students. The belief is that the dances communicate a special kind of knowledge to a certain aspect of our minds. Yet not our intellectual or emotional minds. I've had a little experience with them. I think they do, somehow. I have no way of expressing what is transmitted through the dancing, but it is something, some kind of information.

Mishlove: The Gurdjieff story is that he eventually contacted a secret order of monks in a hidden monastery. While visiting, he studied and learned the methods that he then shared with the world.

Tart: Isn't that romantic?

Mishlove: It is.

Tart: It was an organization supposedly called the Sarmoung Brotherhood. I've never been able to write to the registrar to ask if Gurdjieff got a master's degree from them. He may have made it up or not. Gurdjieff was very insistent that he was teaching ways of development and principles that people had to learn for themselves. The last thing they should do would be to get hung up on his personality. Gurdjieff deliberately obscured a lot of details of his life, including making some of them up. He reasoned by keeping people from trying to trace his bio down, in frustration, they would return to the real work.

Mishlove: Some of his writings are also very dense. The book, *Meetings with Remarkable Men,* is quite approachable, but his other great magnum opus, *Beelzebub's Tales to His Grandson,* is almost impossible.

Tart: Yep, and I'm told it's impossible by design. Gurdjieff thought it held such important teachings, that people needed to understand, and most have no appreciation for what is grasped easily. So, the story is that he would write a chapter in Beelzebub's *Tales* and read it to a group of his students. If they got it, he'd go back and rewrite it to make it denser; harder to follow. Whoa, that's hard, when you value clear writing. I don't pretend to understand *Beelzebub's Tales.*

Mishlove: Also, from a business perspective, no publisher wants to publish a book that's impossible to read. And yet Gurdjieff, as I recall, was a successful author and businessman.

Tart: And a very varied businessman ... from selling rugs to, who knows what sort of deals. Apparently shady sometimes, too. When doing business, he didn't have much respect for ordinary people. Especially if he thought you were motivated by greed. In his mind, it didn't matter if he took advantage of you. That is not an attitude I like.

Mishlove: What drew you to the Gurdjieff work?

Tart: I had been trying to find some kind of spiritual development system. One that would produce spiritual growth and experiences, without much success. I tried to learn various kinds of meditation, mainly from books, and contact with a few teachers. I was a lousy meditator. A few years later I basically gave up meditation. I just decided it required a special talent I did not have. In retrospect, it's like all the meditation instructions say, "First quiet your mind, and then ..." I couldn't get to the "and then" part.

I remember a Tibetan Lama. I once took many classes on meditation from him. He was always talking about the space between thoughts. I thought, what a fascinating concept. What is the space between thoughts? There is no space between minds. There can be a space between thoughts. And I wasn't getting anywhere with the stuff called meditation. Then I came across P. D. Ouspensky's book, *In Search of the Miraculous.* I've recommended it as the best book on Gurdjieff's teachings for a long time. In fact, it is probably a better book than the ones I've written, only different in emphasis, somehow.

Ouspensky was a journalist in Russia. He made his living by writing clearly. He discovered Gurdjieff and wrote about many of his ideas. And he was Gurdjieff's chief disciple for a long time, although eventually they had a falling out. Gurdjieff came back to the West via the Middle East in the 1930s.

Mishlove: He had an institute in Paris. He visited New York, I know.

Tart: Gurdjieff was starting to do work in Russia. The Russian Revolution came along, and he moved. There are still Gurdjieff groups in Russia, apparently. He spent most of the rest of his life teaching in the West. Today there are groups existing, without much publicity, Gurdjieff groups are scattered here and there. Many in these circles have the attitude that if you can't find them, you're not ready for the teachings. This thinking may be a great test.

Mishlove: Occasionally I'm in a public library and I pick up a Gurdjieff book. There is generally a little bookmark inside that states, if you want more information, call this phone number.

Tart: Yeah, because you've passed a preliminary test. You are interested enough to look at a book on Gurdjieff. Now, I think his teachings are profound. My first understanding of this was from a purely intellectual perspective. I read Ouspensky's book, and about half of it I couldn't understand. Gurdjieff talks about the nature of the cosmos and all that. It is teaching so far beyond anybody's ordinary experience; I have no idea whether it's profound truth or total nonsense. So, I don't pay much attention to that part.

Mishlove: And Gurdjieff has a unique language. You must learn the vocabulary.

Tart: Right. That was part of his making you work to learn something. But the other half is about the way the mind functions. And it struck me, he was right about many things. What particularly influenced me was this. One day, while I was at the University of Virginia, teaching, doing some research, I was reading an Ouspensky book. He was describing Gurdjieff's method of becoming more awake or aware. "Waking up" was the vernacular he used. The essence of the method is that ordinarily our attention gets totally absorbed in whatever we're perceiving. So, if I was listening to you or talking to you, I'd be all absorbed in what you're saying and so forth. But Gurdjieff said you must split your attention, so you're also paying attention backwards. You must notice how you're reacting, what you're doing, and what you are taking in from the outside.

So, I was trying to do that while reading it, and for a few seconds, it worked. This was 50 years ago. I couldn't describe at the time what happened, so it's even harder now. I have to say, I woke up. For a few seconds I was in a state of consciousness where somehow it was perfectly clear that my ordinary consciousness was just a dull bunch of conditioned responses. By ordinary standards I was a smart, intellectual, and practical person, yet I wasn't awake. Then I went back to my usual sleep and could think about it intellectually and talk about it. It was years before I could have a moment of the waking experience again.

Mishlove: So, it lasted just a few seconds, and it had a profound impact on you.

Tart: It was so obviously different. I thought of myself as having a stubborn mind; it didn't change easily. But Gurdjieff's primary teaching is, man is asleep. Now, of course, we'd want to make it politically correct today. One might say humans are asleep and all that. What Gurdjieff meant is not that we're asleep in the sense that we are not responsive, but that we live in an internal daydream. This dream-state is distorting our perceptions, including our reactions, and the way we then act back. We sleepwalk through life.

We have enormous amounts of quite specific evidence in ordinary psychology now. For instance, from the clinical psychology courses, I learned a lot about defense mechanisms. When parts of our mind automatically react to distort our perceptions, to protect us from certain feelings and so forth. Gurdjieff spoke about it in a general way, but it was true. In a very real sense, a lot of times we are not home. What Gurdjieff said is, if you live your life in a trance, it's wasted. And he proposed weird cosmological theories about what this did for the evolution of the universe, to turn you into food, basically. Weirdest stuff I've ever read.

Mishlove: Food for the moon, as I recall.

Tart: It made no sense to me. Maybe it was to scare people to say, look, if you don't start training your attention to wake up, your life is not going to be worthwhile. An extreme form of the old saying: the unexamined life is not worth living.

Mishlove: It's also intriguing that his discussion of "man is asleep" occurred roughly at the time Sigmund Freud was developing the notion of the subconscious defense mechanism and psychoanalysis as a cure.

Tart: Freud was getting specific about some of the ways in which we are asleep. This is why I say modern psychology, in a sense. From the Gurdjieffian perspective, Freud developed a lot of the specifics about the ways we are asleep.

Mishlove: Although the cure is very different.

Tart: Yes, the cure is to become normal. Gurdjieff would say your normal culture is asleep, too. You're uncomfortable if you are asleep in a different way than traditions. Everyone wants to be normal. Yet you haven't advanced much just to fit with your society's dreams, distortions and neuroses.

Mishlove: One of the cures you mentioned are the physical, dance-like movements.

Tart: Partly that was training attention. I was just thinking about this recently, as I reran a video of some of the Gurdjieff movements. I remembered the one in the *Meetings with Remarkable Men* movie. I compared it with whirling dervishes. I was thinking, the whirling dervishes, what they do takes some discipline. Their aim is to get into an altered state of consciousness that has mystical significance. The Gurdjieff movements are much more complex. You must be precisely aware, to know exactly when to open your hand, lift your arm, turn your head, and so forth. The movements are training in being precisely present, instant by instant, in the moment. And I think they convey something else, too. Clearly, they are major training in becoming more precisely here.

Mishlove: And not about, for example, going into a trance state.

Tart: No. Gurdjieff would be anti-trance, in a sense. Gurdjieff talked about altered states. The problem is you have to get out of the sleep that you're in. This combined with another one of his ideas: we have three major kinds of intelligence. He named them centers, but I think intelligences would be a better word. One is intellectual. No sweat on that. I held a black belt in talking by the time I was 12. I'm good with words. Another is emotional intelligence. And the third is a body-instinctive kind of intelligence.

Gurdjieff said the problem of almost everyone is only one kind of intelligence is developed.

For instance, many times I was in an emotional situation. I tried to solve it intellectually but that didn't resonate with the realities of the situation. Or some people become centered in this body intelligence. A problem develops and you [physically] push your way through, instead of paying attention to the intellectual or emotional aspects. We are beginning, in psychology, to recognize the value of emotional intelligence. Bodily-instinctive intelligence is wonderful. Gurdjieff says these three intelligences must be reasonably balanced, not perfect. But each must be able to function well, on its own while taking in the world and reasoning in its style. One cannot be so overdeveloped that it knocks out the functioning of the others.

If you reach that level of balanced development the possibility of a much deeper spiritual self becomes real, not just an interesting fantasy. There are higher levels of development. This gets very theoretical. But it does fit into what I think of as a positive framework. Gurdjieff's worldview is that the universe, including its intelligence, is evolving. If you wake up more, you can participate in the evolution of the universe. Rather than, say, a Buddhist kind of thing, where this is samsara. Or it's all illusion and inherent suffering and getting out of here is the important thing rather than evolving. I am a child of the 20th century. Progress and whatnot. I go for evolution.

Mishlove: As a psychologist, especially these days, one might say there are forms of psychotherapy that deal with awakening the body's intelligence. There are many schools of body therapy. Most of them go back to the work of Wilhelm Reich and removing the body's armor, for example. And then there are schools of psychotherapy that deal with the emotions. And there are schools of psychotherapy that are based on cognitive processes.

Tart: Right. Realize rationally that you are being stupid and stop.

Mishlove: But Gurdjieff is doing two things differently, it seems to me. One, he's not a psychotherapist. He's not promising psychotherapy. He's doing it in a completely different context. He is trying to work on the areas simultaneously.

Tart: Yeah. And he is not gentle about it either. His attitude is, if you don't get more awake, your life is a waste. And if you're not willing to work hard on it, too bad. Many people came to him because he was known as a mystic, full of romantic ideas of love and brotherhood and all that. And he believed these supplicants were so out of touch with reality, they didn't have a chance. He'd chase them away. He would do other odd things to train people. There is the story of one Russian refugee living at the Gurdjieff center in France. He apparently was the world's most annoying man. He drove everybody nuts and the students all hated him. The students finally worked up some horrible practical joke involving his false teeth to drive him away. Gurdjieff immediately drove to Paris and offered to pay him to come back. Gurdjieff believed the way the Russian annoyed people gave them incredible opportunities to observe their machinery in action. I might think I'm a calm, easygoing kind of person, but certain situations, oh …

Mishlove: Push your buttons.

Tart: I need the button pushed. If I'm already committed to closely observing myself, then what would be just an annoyance becomes a great opportunity to learn something about my conditioning, my defense mechanisms, et cetera.

Mishlove: You led groups that did this type of work.

Tart: Yes, eventually I led one group; not many of them.

Mishlove: And you attended others.

Tart: Oh, yes. I was involved in several Gurdjieff groups. As happens with many spiritual movements, when the leader dies, different disciples break off. They say, I'm the real successor and those other people don't understand what's going on. So, you must make your choice on which one is the real one. His stuff lends itself to abuse, so there have been very abusive people who claim that they are teaching people to be awake.

Mishlove: One might argue, Gurdjieff himself abused people.

Tart: Yeah. It's like this. If you're dying because your liver is going to explode soon and you won't allow me to cut you open to operate, you will die. I may have to remind you that you're going to die if you don't do something about this. That was his attitude. I don't like that kind of attitude. I'm not that kind of person. I can't be mean to people unless I'm in a very bad state myself. I don't like the way I am when I'm that way. I present Gurdjieff as a much gentler way of inviting change. I encourage people to become more aware of the moment. That's the essence of the work. One begins to bring their consciousness into a precise awareness of what's happening at this moment. When I'm talking to you, what am I doing with my hands? What's the position I'm sitting in? What is that noise in the background? It's not so much that I lose track of what you're saying, but that things are happening now. Some of them may be relevant. Whereas ordinarily I'll have my idea set of who you are and what you're going to say. I'm living in a semi-dream state, with these ideas of what you are like modulating my actual perception of you. I may miss important cues about what's going on in your mind this way.

Mishlove: It seems almost inevitable. You can't pick up everything.

Tart: No, you can't pick up everything. But if you know you can't pick up everything, you're a big jump ahead. Whereas if you just assume you've got it all taken care of and it's your automatic mechanisms working. That's one of the primary ways Gurdjieff insulted some people. He said man is a machine. You don't need to study psychology, you study machines. Push button A, machine B moves in a certain way. That's our conditioning. A machine is more complicated than that, but we are automatic.

Mishlove: But in much of Western behavioral psychology, the whole stimulus-response arc is about exactly that.

Tart: Right. Except the behaviorists were stuck in a sterile view of the universe where there is no spiritual possibility behind beginning to understand what the behavior is. Let me make this more personal. I'm not some kind of Gurdjieff teacher. There's no branch of the Gurdjieff work that's ever authorized me to teach. I've even been thrown out of one or two branches of the Gurdjieff work for questioning some of the things there. But my questioning is usually, I hope, a genuine desire to understand things better. I'm not a very good follower that way. I'm also very interested in Buddhism for the meditative aspects of it. So, I go on Buddhist oriented retreats because meditation is a way of seeing my own internal processes more clearly.

But Buddhism is too isolated. It's like you spend a million hours sitting on a little cushion surrounded by other people sitting on cushions and you may get more mindful of your mental processes in that condition. But then you go out into the world where it's all very different. You forget about it. Whereas the emphasis in Gurdjieff is on developing this quicker, deeper awareness in actual life situations.

Mishlove: I presume meditation is not particularly part of the Gurdjieff work.

Tart: Some of the Gurdjieff work involves some meditation, but the emphasis is on practicing mindfulness in everyday life. Very few people have ever gotten in trouble while they're sitting on a little black cushion.

Mishlove: In fact, the very term, "Gurdjieff work," does imply—and I think Gurdjieff writes about this—the importance of work, of doing, of accomplishing things.

Tart: Right. And of bringing your mindfulness to life. How many mistakes have we all made while we were supposedly sane and conscious? How many times have we looked back and said, how could I have done that thing? It makes no sense. But I did it gustily. Learning to observe yourself, to understand the mechanism, to be more aware, makes a huge difference.

I give a sort of idealistic split between intellect, emotion, body, instinctual and all that. They interact in some ways. For instance, it's the primary way of splitting your attention, so you're taking and seeing and hearing and have some body sensation. Logically, you'd think that makes you more aware of seeing and hearing. But it also makes you more aware of your emotions, because emotions have bodily components.

Mishlove: They're all connected.

Tart: Yeah. So, you pick up aspects of emotions that you might not normally or consciously be aware of, yet they are beginning to control you. By picking them up, you have more choice.

Mishlove: Charley Tart, thank you so much for sharing these reflections. Looking at the Gurdjieff work, one can see it had a real influence in its own day. And now, through people such as yourself, that influence continues to grow.

Tart: I hope so. There's a lot of good stuff in it.

Mishlove: Thank you for being with me, Charley.

Tart: Thank you for a chance to talk about it, Jeff.

10

Education in Parapsychology

~

Recorded on November 10, 2016

Jeffrey Mishlove: Hello and welcome, I'm Jeffrey Mishlove. Today we're going to explore education in parapsychology. With me is Professor Charles Tart, an emeritus professor of psychology at the University of California at Davis, as well as an emeritus professor at the Institute of Transpersonal Psychology.

Welcome, Charley.

Charles Tart: Good to be here, Jeff.

Mishlove: It's a pleasure to be with you. I know we have a long history together going back to the early 1970s, so it's especially nice to be with you.

Tart: I'm sure when you had initially contacted me back then, I gave you my standard letter to discourage you from getting into weird stuff like parapsychology, and you were one of those young idealists who didn't pay any attention to it. Well, that's how I was anyway.

Mishlove: We both were, but we each followed very different paths. You've been in mainstream academia throughout your entire career, which is rare for a parapsychologist.

Tart: It's extremely rare, unfortunately.

Mishlove: I know at least one of your students, Etzel Cardeña, who I believe was a student of yours at Davis, has gone on to become a professor of parapsychology in Sweden.

Tart: Parapsychology and hypnosis, I think, is the special chair that he occupies. But to add a note of realism, he was only able to get that position because the university was bequeathed money by someone who specified that it be for a professor studying parapsychology and hypnosis. It's unlikely that the university on its own would have ever looked for a professor of parapsychology, it's sad to say.

Mishlove: In fact, I think it was the Parapsychology Foundation that approached the University of Southern California with funds to endow a chair, and the university refused to accept it.

Tart: Let me quickly counter this. I think the question of whether we have a spiritual nature or whether, as the materialists say, we're basically all a chemical accident is about the most important question human beings can ask, because it affects our outlook on life. Parapsychology and transpersonal psychology are attempts to bring the power and discipline of science to bear on questions about our nature, so it's not a matter of believing in something spiritual or physical. It's a matter of having evidence indicating that one is probably true, or the other is probably false. It's so important.

If I say to you, Jeff, that I don't need you anymore, so I think I'll kill you for the insurance money. Well, all I've done is stopped some chemical reactions, big deal, if I can get away with it. But if I think there's a chance that we're spiritual beings that are intimately linked and compassion and love are real and important parts of the universe, that changes everything. So, wouldn't it be nice to have some evidence one way or the other? What we're talking about is important, even though, in practice, there are a lot of difficulties.

Mishlove: There are those who say that this is an area that should be relegated to religion or that it's impossible to come up with any evidence. Logically, philosophically, whatever evidence you come up with will fall short.

Tart: One of the ways I like to tease some of my religious friends is by asking them if there has been any progress in religion and spirituality? Are a higher percentage of people who try to become enlightened getting enlightened? Is a higher percentage getting saved? They're taken aback by these questions. Religion is pretty much where it was a thousand years ago—believe it or else—but there has been no progress or experimentation, for instance, regarding what aspects of religion are probably true and what are just cultural artifacts, superstitions, or political power plays. We desperately need to apply our intelligence to this question of whether we are spiritual beings or just animated meat.

Mishlove: These are questions that William James began to explore 130 to 140 years ago, both in terms of psychical research, the scientific and academic study of religion, and developing scientific psychology. He made great progress in his own lifetime and, I would imagine if things had progressed along the outlines that he began to develop, we now would have very active disciplines.

Tart: Yes, very much so, but it didn't work that way.

Mishlove: It didn't work out that way due to the influence of behaviorism. For example, for 50 years, consciousness was almost a taboo subject for psychologists.

Tart: If you ask people the science pecking order, physicists are real scientists because they get exact results. Economy, that's the dismal science. Where are psychologists? They're way down there somewhere with the economists. Psychologists didn't like that, so they tried to make psychology into a socially acceptable science, which meant copying the physical sciences. I've got a white lab coat somewhere that I used to bring out when I had to pose beside my electronic equipment for media people and whatnot. I didn't need a white lab coat to keep the chemical stains off my suit, but there's that desire to belong. As one of my professors once said in graduate school, it's only been a hundred years since they let us out of the philosophy department. As psychologists, we're afraid they'll send us back, and that tells you where philosophers are in the pecking order among scientists. They're way down there.

Mishlove: They are way down.

Tart: One famous scientist put it as something like, scientists need philosophers like birds need ornithologists.

Mishlove: I know the philosophers have a different point of view.

Tart: They have a different point of view, but they don't do any experiments, and they can't make any nuclear weapons to threaten the rest of us with. Now, our attitude about philosophy is stupid because philosophers can contribute to understanding what we're doing. When a field of science runs into some crisis and things are just not making sense anymore, then they're liable to start thinking about philosophy and what kind of questions to ask and how they ask them, so it's important.

But you're right saying behaviorism threw consciousness out of psychology. It was so strange, predicting behavior, the stuff you could see. But even after it had been around for more than 50 years by the time I was in graduate school, it was quite clear that if you wanted to predict what somebody was going to do next—and that's the criterion for a scientific theory that works—the best thing to do is not look at their behavior, but to ask them what they would do next. It's useful to tap into their consciousness.

Mishlove: An interesting thing is that consciousness is where psychology started. The methodology of the early experimental psychologists was introspection. Look inside your mind and tell me what you see. That line of research was pretty much dropped.

Tart: For good reasons. It had major flaws in it. For one thing, there was no real understanding that it's hard to observe your mind because it's going a mile a minute. I remember, for instance, when I was trying to learn meditation from a Tibetan Lama, Tarthang Tulku. He used to talk about finding the space between thoughts, and I thought it was a fascinating idea, the space between thoughts. But there is no space between my thoughts, zip, zip, this, that, the other thing. It's hard to observe yourself. In the meditative traditions, they talk about people who can understand how the mind works because they've practiced for five thousand or ten thousand hours. A trained observer in early psychology was somebody who, comparatively, had only 10 hours of training so they didn't know how to observe. There was tremendous authoritarianism, too. A lot of study was happening in Germany, and Herr Dr. Professor knew how the mind worked and had some assistants to make observations to prove that point, and your job depended on Herr Dr. Professor liking you. So, there was all sorts of bias.

Mishlove: It's intriguing to me that the field of psychical research, a term still used today, and is the forerunner of parapsychology, got off the ground formally in 1882. That's around the same time that psychology was established as an independent discipline from philosophy. The two of them were operating in parallel for a while, and there were some great contributions from the early psychical researchers. But over time, parapsychology and psychical research got relegated to a fringe position within academia, and psychology, excluding the paranormal, became mainstream.

Tart: There were many reasons for it. We were afraid they'd send us back to the philosophy department. We wanted to be accepted as real scientists, and that means we had to look and talk like the real scientists who were all materialists. We had to become materialists, and materialists had immediately ruled out everything psychic. Take, for instance, a central idea in any spiritual discipline or religion: prayer. From a materialist viewpoint, what is prayer but talking to yourself. If you talk out loud, the sound may get around to the walls of the room but not past that. If you pray in your own mind, it doesn't even get that far. So, prayer is a waste of time. Maybe it'll make you feel better.

But here comes psychical research and parapsychology investigating telepathy and starting to collect evidence that one human mind can pick up information that is in another human mind. They could be outside the room, a mile away, or a hundred miles away. Oh, wait a minute. If prayer involves telepathy, maybe we can't dismiss it as just talking to yourself though sometimes that's what it is. Perhaps we have a glimpse of a mechanism whereby prayer could get information from one place to another.

Mishlove: Suppose you have a student today who is interested in exploring this further, would like to do research, and become a professional expert on the power of prayer from a scientific point of view. How would you advise them to proceed?

Tart: I have an almost standard procedure which unfortunately starts by my asking them if they are independently wealthy. Because if you can take this as a hobby and support yourself, there are a lot of things you could do. But if you must earn a living, you've got to look like a mainstream scientist: get a degree in a graduate school, get grants to support your research and so forth. If you show an interest in parapsychological matters, you probably won't even be accepted in a graduate program. I know of some of the few academic parapsychologists, for instance, who if a student applied to their graduate program and mentioned their research on parapsychology, thought they were not all that bright. Since graduate schools only take a fraction of those who apply, those with that interest don't even get in.

It seems stupid to me, but I've always had to advise people that if they have these interests, two things must happen. They must have conventional interests too, so they can work in some aspect of psychology or physics or something else and it'll be satisfying and economically feasible. But through graduate school and even through much of their academic career, to be very careful who they talk to. Because a lot of people who are designated as scientists, who are supposed to be open-minded and go just by evidence, reject the very possibility of telepathy, prayer, or anything parapsychological. These materialists will attack them for making them uncomfortable by mentioning these possibilities. It is so stupid to tell graduate students to be very careful what they talk about with their professors.

Mishlove: They will attack you for making *them* uncomfortable.

Tart: Yes, exactly.

Mishlove: When people come to me, I give them the same good, solid advice. But, at the same time, I feel obliged to tell people that I didn't follow that advice myself. I was neither independently wealthy nor did I have and apply any kind of credentials or expertise in another field. I do have a master's degree in criminology, but I haven't worked professionally in that area.

Tart: Some people might think you're a criminal for promoting parapsychology.

Mishlove: Some people indeed might. And one could say I'm a deviant, in that regard.

Tart: Yes.

Mishlove: But I think, if you look at the population, everybody's a little bit deviant in one way or another. I haven't seen anybody who's perfectly normal in every respect.

Tart: Well, I was just like you. I didn't follow this good advice, because I have a strong sense of right and wrong, and I have enormous respect for the scientific method, and that requires you to be completely honest and open about the data, the stuff you can observe, and your thinking about it. But, luckily, I had a lot of more mainstream interests too. When I got into graduate school, I focused my work on dream research, which was a hot new topic then when we discovered there were brainwave correlates of dreaming. I kept at least two-thirds of my research on things like dream or hypnosis research, which were relatively respectable compared to parapsychology. But I didn't hide the parapsychology, and I suffered a great deal for it. I don't regret it because that's me. I'm honest about my interests.

Mishlove: And despite all the suffering—and I'm sure it was quite real for you—you still managed to obtain tenure, and you are now an emeritus professor.

Tart: That's right, but I wasted at least a year or two of my career, when I start thinking of all the times I had to defend against attacks. Now what was strange is that at my university, there were a lot of people who pointed to my research as an example of how the university upheld the principle of academic freedom. If you're doing quality research, you can do it in any subject. Then there were a lot of other people who worked to get me fired. Luckily, they didn't succeed. So, the advice I give people is to find some conventional area of science that would be relevant to parapsychology. Psychology is an obvious one, or physics. Find one that's interesting enough that you'll enjoy because you've got to work hard to get through graduate school. But then keep the interest in parapsychological stuff muted until you get tenure. And let's hope they keep giving people tenure. Administrators would love to get rid of it because it's easier to fire people, unfortunately.

Mishlove: Yeah, there are big changes going on in academia.

Tart: Yes. And I hope that the culture changes in a way that my cautionary words become obsolete and quaint as soon as possible.

Mishlove: I'm doing these interviews, Charley, because I think the day is going to come, maybe a hundred years from now, when mainstream colleges and universities around the world will have departments of parapsychology or something comparable, just as they have psychology and philosophy and criminology and other specializations now. I think these conversations will be useful for people when that day arrives.

Tart: Let me give you another example of why psychologists particularly are irrationally opposed to parapsychology. Partly, it's because parapsychology is not a material science, so it doesn't look like real science. Also, standard psychological experiments mean that you control sensory communication, and what the subject knows about the experiment, so your opinions and biases don't matter. But if you allow for telepathy then a subject might find out what's supposed to happen.

One of my areas of research was the question of experimenter bias like Robert Rosenthal's research where he told some teachers that certain students were bright, and others were kind of dumb. Supposedly, those teachers treated everybody the same, but the achievement of the students varied enormously. Bias can control the results of an experiment. I think the possibility of telepathy as another way of treating bias is frightening to most psychologists. So, they ignore telepathy, as if it doesn't exist but that's not realistic.

Mishlove: The implications of this weak phenomenon are still very significant if it's influencing social science and behavioral research.

Tart: Many of the findings of psychology have the same size and magnitude as what you get in ESP experiments. That's scary. I don't have many good answers regarding the problem of bias. My main answer is, "Know thyself." If you know what your biases are, then you might be able to reduce their influence. If you just assume you're an objective experimenter, then your biases could run riot.

Mishlove: I know there's a big movement in the social and behavioral sciences now to focus on what are called "questionable research practices," and that a great deal of conventional research is now being called into question.

Tart: It should be.

Mishlove: Experiments are hard to replicate because one study will contradict another. It's not nearly as neat and clean cut as it often appears in your introductory freshman textbooks.

Tart: These experiments are well below the quality level of where parapsychology experiments have been for the last half century. Many of these questionable research practices were things considered by parapsychologists to begin with like selectively throwing out some data because it didn't make sense. Parapsychologists realized long ago that you've got to account for all the data. Another requirement for success in parapsychology is being very, very honest and ready to be disappointed when experiments don't work out or to question beliefs. And, you're going to have to put up with a lot of crap from colleagues who should be open minded.

Mishlove: I think part of the reason for that is, as we've been hinting, parapsychology challenges established paradigms. Parapsychology requires people, if they take it seriously, to rethink a lot of things they thought they could take for granted.

Tart: I'm glad we're doing consciousness research at last, but the dominant view is neurophysicalism, which is that consciousness is produced by the action of neurons in the brain. All the parapsychological phenomena like telepathy, clairvoyance, and remote viewing says the mind is not limited to the brain. The brain is still important, but I like, as a working hypothesis, Aldous Huxley's characterization of the brain as a reducing valve. Our mind, in some spiritual sense, can take in everything about the universe from everywhere, but that would be extremely distracting. When you're driving your car, you don't want to hear voices, you want to focus on things that have immediate relevance. So, the neurophysicalism paradigm, which is dominant, says if you get the right brain scanner, you'll explain everything about consciousness.

An analogy I often use regarding the mind is a car and a driver. You can see what the car does, how it is built, and why it works the way it does. But sometimes, the driver gets out of the car and does different things than what a car can do or what a car and driver together can do. You must look at the driver alone too. Parapsychology is ultimately going to be the study of the "non-physical" driver. I put quotes around it because I can't define non-physical very well. But there's something else than the physical, and that's super important. If we have a spiritual nature, then we should be focusing on that instead of what can I do biologically to make myself happy and get away with it.

Mishlove: You're talking basically about questioning metaphysical assumptions that are implicit in society. Since we've talked about the influence of the behaviorists, there's also the positivists in philosophy who have argued that metaphysical assumptions of any kind are out of bounds. They should never be discussed at all. I think Wittgenstein said at one point they should be passed over in silence.

Tart: When I can't follow a conversation, I think people should stop talking about the things I don't know. But that's about my limits, not about reality. I also want to object to your use of "metaphysical assumptions" because that sounds very abstract and has nothing to do with ordinary life. These assumptions do control our lives. Some of them are built in as biological control apps, but a lot of them are cultural beliefs that control how we perceive, think, and react to things. They're not just metaphysical in some abstract sense.

Mishlove: Charley, as we wrap up this interview, it seems to me that one of the main themes is that for a young person wanting to go into this field, and I suspect there are thousands out there ...

Tart: Oh, I know. I get letters from them.

Mishlove: They need to know there are going to be many obstacles. I'm reminded of the time I interviewed Joseph Campbell, and I asked him the advice he offers to young people. He smiled, and he said, "Follow your passion." I think you must have a passion, or you won't get through all the obstacles.

Tart: That's right, but don't assume you can make a living just by writing books about it either because the situation for authors is miserable nowadays. Most people will still have to earn a living, so you've got to take that into account. And don't sell out.

Mishlove: Just parenthetically, I might say in my case, it helped that I had an entrepreneurial spirit and was willing to kind of make my own way in the world. I suffered a lot of knocks along the way but kept going.

Tart: And that gave you a freedom to explore these things that you wouldn't have had otherwise.

Mishlove: I'm still going as this moment expresses itself, and I love it.

Tart: You first interviewed me 30 or 40 years ago, but I must say you don't seem to have slowed down the slightest.

Mishlove: It's so great to be with you, Charley. Thanks so much.

Tart: Thank you, Jeff.

11

Science as a Spiritual Path

~

Recorded on November 10, 2016

Jeffrey Mishlove: Hello and welcome. I'm Jeffrey Mishlove. Today, we will look at science as a spiritual path with Professor Charles Tart. Welcome, Charley.

Charles Tart: Good to be here, Jeff. Nice, tough topic for discussion today.

Mishlove: It's an extraordinarily interesting topic because I know we can, and will, go into great depth about why science is, in fact, a spiritual path. I imagine if you asked most scientists, they would scoff at the idea.

Tart: Most scientists have bought into a totally materialistic view of the world. We are here only because of subatomic particles bumping into each other in a certain way, purely by chance, a zillion years ago. So, we happened to end up here and it all means nothing. The conventional ideas about spirituality and religion are dropped. Yeah, officially, science totally rejects the idea. They do it in a sensible way by simply saying, we have expert knowledge in dealing with the material stuff. We don't know anything about the spiritual world, so we won't talk about it. But it often extends into a put-down of the spiritual. I am putting myself down at the beginning of this interview because I can speak as an expert about science. I'm good at it. I've been doing it for a long time.

Mishlove: You have hundreds of published papers in scientific journals.

Tart: It's an objective criterion. I know this stuff. As to spirituality, I consider myself a spiritual seeker. I'm not an accomplished spiritual person, by any means. But I'm trying. I think a lot of people are in this position, so hopefully, I can share something useful.

Mishlove: Let me ask: can one be a materialist and an atheist and still walk a spiritual path?

Tart: What would spiritual mean in that case?

Mishlove: It might mean seeking the truth. You could be a seeker.

Tart: Well, you can use the word spiritual, in a very broad sense in that way, and it would be a noble sort of thing to do. But I wouldn't want to broaden [the term] spiritual quite that much. To me, when I use the term spiritual, I'm using it roughly. We can only do it roughly these days. There is the obvious material world here. We know a great deal about it, and yet we believe there is some other real level of existence. One that is more important than this physical level and from which come values, on how we should live our life. Love at the material level: some people explain it away as a hormonal surge through your body. At the spiritual level, people might say we know something about love. The spirit of the universe or God or whatever you want to say radiates love or is love. That's very different. So, I can't define spirituality precisely. We don't know enough, but that's kind of the commonsense distinction.

Mishlove: I certainly have heard people say, about Buddhism, that Buddhism is atheistic and materialistic, but also a spiritual path.

Tart: That's an incorrect statement as I understand Buddhism. Atheistic usually means you say there is no God. Buddhism says, oh yeah, there are lots of gods. They can't help you get enlightened because they're not enlightened themselves. Maybe they'll do you a favor occasionally, but you can't rely on them for anything. *You* must clear up the obstructions in your own mind that keep you from being enlightened. So not atheistic in the denial of existence sense.

Mishlove: No, but atheistic in the sense that whatever these entities are, they're not permanent; they're not ultimate.

Tart: Right. The Buddhism approach is this: we have the capacity to move beyond suffering; to be very happy. But for many reasons, we basically do all sorts of unskillful and stupid things that create all sorts of suffering. We must learn what those things are and stop doing them. Then the suffering will stop. That's an oversimplification, of course. As I often remind people, I'm not a Buddhist scholar either, even though I've gotten teaching from a lot of Buddhists.

Mishlove: I know there are many different interpretations of Buddhism. Once, years ago, I interviewed someone who, I think, is an old friend of yours, Walter Anderson. He wrote a book on Buddhism and argued that the Buddha was no different than a postmodern deconstructionist philosopher, which is close to being an atheist materialist.

Tart: That's one way of looking at some of what the Buddha did. He said that things are compounded, and if you can break them down into parts, they don't have as much power over you. But I think he had a few other things in mind, too. But understand this: There are people who make me out as some kind of authority on Buddhism. Compared to the man in the street, I guess I am an authority. But compared to a Buddhist scholar or certified Buddhist teachers, I know nothing. Anything I say about Buddhism can be contradicted by the actual practices of some group that is officially Buddhist. What I speak is a Western take on Buddhism, most important for us.

Mishlove: As you said earlier, you're a scientist.

Tart: Yes, I'm very much a scientist.

Mishlove: A credentialed scientist.

Tart: I can make a connection there, too. The Buddha did give one teaching which allows science to be applied to Buddhism. The Buddha gave a teaching he called the teaching to the Kalamas, some native group in India. He basically said, don't believe anything because some authority figure tells you it's true, or because it's a long-held, hallowed belief. Anything you hear, test it. If it works out for your good and fits reality, good, keep it. If not, let it go. Well, that's kind of the essence of science. We have theories and beliefs, but those are just our best attempts to make sense of things. Keep going back to what you can see about reality and form your beliefs on that basis. Be open to change as you learn new things.

Mishlove: So, in one sense, if we think of this as a description of science itself, science then becomes a spiritual path, constantly adjusting itself to the face of evidence, in the search for truths that are more permanent.

Tart: Yes. I think of it that way. I was raised conventionally as a Lutheran. My grandmother took me to Sunday school and church. Grandmothers are the source of unconditional love. So, if it was good enough for her, it was good enough for me. When I got to be a teenager and thinking for myself and began learning science, I started to question a lot of that. But one of the things I was taught, that I still take as a working hypothesis, is that God is supremely intelligent. And we are made in God's image. That seems to mean, we should be intelligent. When you're a little kid you can get away with it. Later, you learn you're not supposed to apply your intelligence to organized religions or question doctrine. From a scientific perspective, I would say religion starts because people have spiritual experiences, all very important, and we love to explain things. We are not comfortable unless we explain things. So, a theory is made about the experience. That's the first step of science. Something happens, you make up a theory. You keep testing the theory. But what occurs in some religions is it becomes holy doctrine. You must believe it or you're a heretic. And so, the inquiry stops. In a sense, I'm advocating an experimental spirituality in religion. What happened? What theories can you create from the experience? And then, can these theories be tested or improved, modified, and tweaked?

Mishlove: You seem to be saying that if someone is truly a scientist and willing to examine the data, particularly the data about consciousness, it's going to point them in the direction of non-physical spiritual realms.

Tart: Yes, if they will look at all the data we have about consciousness. People have experiences, events happen which do not fit into an "it's all physical" framework. If you're truly being scientific, you must admit there is data I have to make sense of, and not because it doesn't fit. But it couldn't have happened; I'll forget all about it. Avoidance is prejudice. Yet it is very common. A scientist is usually someone technically trained within a particular discipline, and not trained to question the basics, or the paradigm of the discipline. That's all right in one way. Scientists are specialists in tweaking things, but if you get stuck within a particular explanatory framework, you're not able to look at the data carefully.

Mishlove: Furthermore, practically every scientist earns a PhD degree, a Doctor of Philosophy. The whole point of philosophy is to question your assumptions.

Tart: I think that got forgotten somewhere, didn't it? I do that all the time. For instance, I try to practice a basic form of Buddhist meditation usually called Vipassana or insight meditation. I can't say that, oh gosh, wonderful spiritual experiences happen to me, because they don't. But what I do see are deeper insights to the way my mind works: assumptions I make about the way things should be. Not only do I discover assumptions I have made, but I notice my mind is pushing or pulling slightly on my perception to fit the beliefs I already have. That's not science. It's comforting to have your beliefs reinforced, but if they lose touch with reality, you're in trouble.

Mishlove: It seems in politics and religion the mind actively looks for events in the physical world to reinforce our beliefs.

Tart: We have an old-fashioned belief that there are two kinds of mental functioning. One is perception: we take in the world as it is. I see you sitting there, I hear your voice and it's sort of high fidelity. I might think about it as something different. But modern psychology and neurology show that perception is high-speed automatic thinking. There are filters taking in my visual perception of you, hearing your words, and so forth. Most of the time, these filters operate reasonably accurately. I don't step in front of cars and get run down. However, they can seriously distort our view of the world, especially as you do not realize the filters are a form of thinking and belief.

Mishlove: I often hear materialistic scientists say that science gives them a sense of wonder about nature itself and how awesome it is.

Tart: That's good. A sense of wonder can lead you to look at things more closely. But what science can also do is make you believe, "I'm a superior person. I'm not like the ordinary uneducated masses out there. I understand how the world works, "based on a certain degree of truth. This thinking very quickly inflates your ego and makes you blind.

Mishlove: I don't know of any tradition in science that says, "Learn to put aside your ego."

Tart: Exactly. This is particularly true in the case of psychology. It's assumed we are objective scientists. I never had any courses in graduate school, for instance, learning how to observe the workings of my own mind and its bias. Yet while investigating unusual subject matter, like altered states or parapsychology, I have found it important to know my biases because they affect the way I do the experiment.

Mishlove: When you talk about science as a spiritual discipline, I get the impression you are thinking about a science of the future, one not yet embodied.

Tart: Yes. It's what science could be. The basic method of science starts with curiosity. That's a kind of skepticism. You are not happy with your understanding of a subject. You'd like to understand better. You are curious: why do things do that? So, then you start by observing. If you're intelligent, you realize you are probably a biased and inadequate observer. So, are there ways of observing better? Are there instruments I can develop, if it's of the physical world? Are there mental techniques I can develop if I'm trying to observe how the mind works, for instance? So, you get data. Data is always primary. Then you come up with a theory about it because we love to come up with theories, and then we fall in love with the theories. But this is where science has a very strong discipline that says, if you want your theory to be considered scientific, the predictions must be testable. If there are no testable predictions, it is not science. So, then you must test. If the test verifies your theory, you may want to go on refining it. But if it doesn't work, it's too bad even though your theory is elegant, involving quarks, mesons, block universes, and all the fashionable buzzwords. It doesn't work. You must come up with something new. You keep cycling this around and gradually better and better ideas come. Can one apply this to the spiritual phenomena that constitute the basis of most religions? I think so. What happens? What affects what happens? And so on and so forth. It's a fascinating challenge and it will improve our lives when we achieve success.

Let me elaborate: improve our lives. For example, religions tell us to love our neighbor. That is hard, especially when your neighbors are obnoxious. I find most religions are kind of lightweight when it comes to telling you *how* to love your neighbor. There are certain spiritual experiences people have recorded, at an incredibly deep level through the ages, of a feeling of oneness and love for one another. It's no big deal for me to love you. You and I are one. You and I are one with everybody else.

Mishlove: In other words, there is a certain state of consciousness you can enter that is a natural way of perceiving the world.

Tart: Then it becomes easy and sensible to become a good person. And contribute to harmony in the world instead of, well, I should be nice even though those no-goodniks don't deserve it.

Mishlove: In the mid-1970s, you achieved a certain amount of fame through your writings and research.

Tart: Maybe infamy.

Mishlove: You're still infamous and famous for a paper published, as I recall, in *Science* when you were a young scholar, on state-specific research. As I think about our discussion now, this is what we are talking about here, isn't it?

Tart: We assume that there is ordinary, normal consciousness and that it is *the* best possible state for a mind to work in. Any change is considered nuts, crazy and dumb, something like that. But the way your mind works is strongly channeled by the social conditioning you were raised on in your youth. It's very good at helping you pass for normal and getting along in normal life. But it is a specialized state.

I was giving a lecture once about how different states of consciousness may work better for different things. I reached into my pockets—I wish I had them now—and I pulled out a pair of pliers that I held in one hand and a screwdriver in the other hand. And I said, okay, how many people think the pair of pliers is the better tool? A bunch of hands went up. How many people think the screwdriver is better? Hands went up. Then they started faltering as everybody stood around and said, better for what? Pliers are better for some things and a screwdriver is better for others. I then realized that consciousness could present as different states, much like different tools: good for some things and not for others. Becoming stuck in any one state of consciousness—a hammer is a great tool, but can you fix everything in your house with a hammer, like the TV set? Hammers are not good for TV sets.

Mishlove: In the past, it was thought there were only a handful, or less, of states of consciousness. You were awake or you were asleep, or you were dreaming, basically.

Tart: Yeah. It's a nice and simple thing. You were sane or you were crazy, i.e., the other characterization. But it's more complicated than this. We can go into detail sometime. But for example, take emotions. Any weak emotion is considered an emotion within an ordinary state of consciousness. I'm a little bothered by that notion but pleased by this sort of thing. When any emotion becomes strong, I think, in this way you perceive change. And it becomes the way you think of change as a new kind of whole. If I were in a state of rage, I might say, why do you have this damn statue here? You know, it is ugly. It is obvious to me as an immediate perceptual fact that it's ugly. Well, the rage state of consciousness has changed how my perceptual thinking works.

We are just beginning to realize that emotions can trigger different, altered states of consciousness. Some emotions can trigger you into something that may lead to spiritual experiences. That's one of the ways, perhaps, of how we learn to be good instead of being told to be good. There is a wide-open frontier here in how to use our minds better. Which app do you boot up?

Mishlove: I get the impression that normal waking consciousness, for some people the gap between their norm and a state, let's say, of love and compassion is very wide. For others, it may be very slight. It might just take the smallest little nudge to trigger a feeling of love and compassion.

Tart: Yes. In many cases this gives them a great advantage in life. In other cases, it puts them at a great disadvantage. So, for instance, let's say the gap between ordinary consciousness and rage is very small. Most of the time, they will get into a lot of trouble. These people may take offense at ridiculous slights. Sometimes it may save their lives: If you attack immediately when somebody is attacking you. They may not stop to think about it. You must learn how to use the tool you need. Then you must learn how to use the tool skillfully, to offer that analogy again.

Mishlove: So, science as a spiritual path would require scientists to pay attention, moment by moment, to their states of consciousness.

Tart: Even when you think and believe an experiment is being handled in an objective fashion, what are you communicating? I'll give you an example. I was involved in hypnosis research for many years. There was a big question as to whether hypnosis is an altered state of consciousness or are people suggestible to some extent. Do they just go along with stuff? We had a standard way of testing people's response to suggestions. Our team staged an important experiment. We gave suggestibility tests. Some people were hypnotized first and others, you would chat with them for 10 minutes, instead of initiating the hypnosis procedure. Well, I was an experimenter in this trial—it was a multi laboratory experiment—and I noticed something. When I hypnotized somebody, first, I didn't give the suggestibility test quite the same way. If we only chatted, I'd say something like, hold out your arm and imagine you're holding something heavy with it. Then ask, what would it be like if your arm was getting tired. If I had hypnotized them first, it would be subtle, but [*speaking more slowly and more quietly*] hold out your arm and imagine something heavy, there, pressing down. Well, if you give the test differently, you will get a different [result]. And it will have nothing to do with whether they are hypnotized, or not. This is experimental bias.

Mishlove: The subtlety in your voice would be hard to instrumentalize or operationalize, scientifically.

Tart: I noticed it in myself. I presented this at a laboratory meeting. The other experimenters thought, oh, Charley, always morbidly introspective. We are objective scientists. We do this. I said, okay, if it's true, then you won't mind if I put a microphone in the laboratory and record the experimenters while giving the suggestibility test. Then give it to judges, who don't know the subject's condition, and let them guess [whether] the person has been hypnotized or not. The judges picked up on it extremely well. The experimenters were all biased, a total unknown. The team had to repeat the whole experiment, using a tape-recorded test to ensure the testing would always be done the same way.

How often do we do that in life? A doctor can ask you about your condition and, by subtle intonations in their voice, kind of push you one way or the other. You're thinking about reporting it and whatnot. Same thing on the spiritual side of things. Somebody can tell you that love is what you need to develop. There would be a way to say it. Fortunately, I cannot think of how to demonstrate this idea, that would make it clear enough. And a sinner like you probably isn't going to do it. But you should develop love and, oh yeah, it is easy and natural to do so.

Mishlove: Right. Take this step with me. We can invite ourselves or we can kind of push a person in a way that they may resist the push and go in the other direction.

Tart: When I've trained graduate students, I have tried to impress on them the importance of knowing your biases. Learning to pick up on your moods and feelings and how it might affect what you're doing is vital to a scientist. I don't know how successful I've been with them.

Mishlove: But there are areas of science where this is essential. For example, field research in anthropology or field research in the social sciences. In general, where it's taught, as noted by George Herbert

Mead in the 1930s, it's crucial to know your personal biases. You must lay them out right away.

Tart: You may not know you have them until you see what happens in the results. For instance, if you're polling and you are dressed in a certain way, some people will immediately identify you as somebody they don't like. Even though you are just asking an objective question, do you like this or that, the results become skewed right then and there.

Mishlove: Well, this has been a fascinating discussion. It gives me a lot of insight on the potential for science in the future.

Tart: Oh, yes. I think science and spirituality can eventually help one another become more effective. So that, in the future, when I tease people with this question, has there been any progress in spirituality in the last couple of centuries? I hope the answer will be yes.

Mishlove: And I do sometimes hear people use a term that, when I first heard it, made chills go up and down my spine.

Tart: What was that?

Mishlove: Spiritual science.

Tart: I'm not saying that spirituality is all going to be explained away by some kind of cold science. I'm saying that science can be opened by spirituality. Spirituality can get more accurate and effective by the proper use of science.

Mishlove: Dr. Charles Tart, what a pleasure to share this half hour with you. Thank you so much for being with me.

Tart: The pleasure is mine also.

Mishlove: And (addressing the audience) thank you all for being with us.

12

Altered States of Consciousness

~

Recorded on November 10, 2016

Jeffrey Mishlove: Hello and welcome. I'm Jeffrey Mishlove. Our topic today is altered states of consciousness. Professor Charles Tart, an emeritus professor of psychology at the University of California at Davis and an emeritus professor with the Institute of Transpersonal Psychology. Dr. Tart has authored many books. His anthology called *Altered States of Consciousness*, published in 1969, put the phrase on the map. As a matter of fact, I recall arriving in Berkeley that year. His book was a must-read for every college student at the time. I saw it everywhere. His other titles include *States of Consciousness; Open Mind, Discriminating Mind; Waking Up*, and *Learning to Use Extrasensory Perception.*

Welcome again, Charley.

Charles Tart: Hi Jeff.

Mishlove: Pleasure to be with you. It's obvious that the interest in altered states of consciousness, which was so intense back in 1969 when your book came out, was largely because of the drug culture on college campuses. And I should mention, you authored a book in that era titled, *On Being Stoned.*

Tart: Yeah, a couple of years later.

Mishlove: You took a very serious psychological survey of the experiences reported by marijuana users.

Tart: I was amazed by people's reactions to marijuana. They talked about the terrible things it did. So, I looked in the scientific literature, and what did it do? Well, it made your eyes red. It made you hungry and might affect your blood pressure slightly. But importantly, it earned you a major risk of going to jail. People taking a risk of going to jail for their eyes to get red? Nobody had done much research then on what happens to people's consciousness under the influence. And why marijuana made them want to do it. So, I did a straightforward survey.

Mishlove: As I recall, the major finding was that things look better, sound better, taste better.

Tart: Yeah, *the munchies.* Increased eating happens because foods taste better. People were paying attention to sensory qualities, of all sorts. Instead of, you know, the senses bringing us information. We were busy in the executive office making decisions and thinking. There are many other very interesting effects, too. I also hoped that my work would be totally outmoded within a few years because I did a relatively small survey: only 150 experienced pot users. But now that I showed it could be done, I expected somebody to survey thousands of people; get encyclopedic knowledge. It didn't happen though.

Mishlove: No, your book is still, after so many decades, an authoritative study.

Tart: Not quite because I think marijuana use has changed considerably since then. When I did the study, for instance, almost all the experienced users would say, "You don't drink when you're smoking marijuana. Maybe a little wine for the taste, but you don't drink." Then ten years later it was very common for people to drink heavily while doing it. Alcohol wipes out a lot of the marijuana effects. So different things began happening. But it illustrated an important point. A drug may encourage physiological changes, but what happens to your consciousness depends a great deal on what people do with the changes. So, for instance, it was common knowledge that a lot of people smoked marijuana and nothing happened. Their friends thought they were stoned. Their friends thought they were in an altered state. They didn't notice anything. Then they finally learned to shift their perception and realized the altered state.

But they needed the psychological effects to modulate the physiological effects that it produced.

Mishlove: Your classic anthology talks about ten different kinds of altered states: dreams, hypnosis ... In fact, there's a fascinating chapter, as I recall, on mutual hypnosis.

Tart: Oh yeah. That was something I pioneered because there was hardly any research. In hypnosis, there is the idea that a special relationship or rapport exists between the subject and the hypnotist. I started thinking, well, if that rapport exists and it is important, could you increase it? If A hypnotized B, but while B was hypnotized, B hypnotized A, and then A deepened B, and B deepened A. I was able to do a few sessions like that with a couple of people who were reasonably hypnotically talented. It was fabulous. They fell into very unusual states of consciousness, more than just ordinary hypnosis.

Mishlove: I believe all around the country then, colleges began to have courses on altered states of consciousness.

Tart: When I published that book, there was very little information available about altered states from a scientific perspective. But I had read from many unusual sources while following my interest. So, I thought, let me put it together. The book made an impact. Then people saw, oh, we could have a course on this. We have a textbook now. I still get email, occasionally, from somebody who says, "50 years ago I read *Altered States of Consciousness*, and it changed my life. I began realizing what was possible."

Mishlove: The basic message being there is more to life than just everyday waking consciousness. It becomes kind of humdrum compared to the possibilities of altered states.

Tart: Well, I want to get more specific now. I no longer talk about ordinary consciousness. I talk about consensus consciousness. That is, the way our mind functions is strongly shaped by the culture we were raised in. We notice things that another culture might ignore. We are excited by some things that aren't exciting to another culture or vice versa. Every culture's consciousness is reasonably good at dealing with reality. If not, the culture would become nonexistent. But every culture also has blind spots and psychopathology. What some cultures think is a great way to live would be seen as quite pathological by others. Take, for instance, the ability to go into an altered state of consciousness. If a young kid shows that their eyes glaze over and then they talk about strange things that happen, we send them to a doctor or to a minister to get exorcised. In some more basic human cultures, they might say, ah, maybe he's got a problem or maybe he's got the talent to become a shaman. Let's send him to a shaman for training and see what happens. Use those potentialities, instead of, it's crazy and let's get rid of it.

Mishlove: Now, since we're talking about altered states, I need to mention the movie, *Altered States*.

Tart: Ah, yes. They didn't come to ask anything about it, but some of my stuff was in there.

Mishlove: Yeah, I'm going to show a little clip from that movie because you are mentioned.

Tart: Ah, yes.

Mishlove: I think it's interesting to reflect historically on the cultural impact of your work.

*–Clip from the film **Altered States**–*

> **Actor William Hurt:** There's very little literature on this kind of research. There are some good people in the field: Tart, Ornstein, Deikman, but most are radical, hip stuff, drug culture, apologias. Obviously, the first thing to do is set up some sensible methodology. Let's see if we can't study these experiences under controlled, laboratory conditions. It will not interfere with the work we're doing with Hobart.

> **Actor playing Arthur:** Oh, what are we getting into? I do sensory deprivation, isolation studies. I mean, you know, where will we be going with the tank stuff?

> **Actor William Hurt:** We're not writing up a grant, Arthur. It's strictly bootlegging; just for kicks. I figure as long as we've got the use of this tank, let's play around with it. Let's find out where it takes us. It's fascinating stuff, Arthur. I think we've got to get into it.

–End of Clip–

Tart: The book was a scientific bestseller. Usually with scientific anthologies, a hundred copies sold in this culture, is doing good. *Altered States* sold over 100,000 copies because people were desperate for the information. They didn't like the idea of weird things happening, maybe nice or possibly crazy. The Information from the experts was sketchy, "Oh, I think that's crazy. Don't go there."

Mishlove: The plot of that movie is that a college professor gets deeply interested in altered states and acquires supernormal powers.

Tart: Right, a little more exciting than what happened in my laboratory.

Mishlove: You began your work by researching dreams.

Tart: Yeah, I have been interested in dreams all my life. When I was a kid, I used to have interesting dreams sometimes. Often, I wondered, "well, what are they?" I go to bed and there are some blank spots and then I am in this other world, doing things. I wake up the next morning and ask the adults about it. They can't tell me anything useful. They say, "Oh, it's just a dream." This is our culture's way of saying, it is unimportant. No need to bother to think about it, and so forth. Then as I got older, and started reading psychological ideas: Freud, Jung, others, I began thinking about the possible significance of dreams. Then later, I came across information suggesting hypnosis might be used to influence dreams. But it was very old literature, buried in obscure places. It was among some of my psychotherapy research papers. It wasn't clear to me how real this idea was, but it got me interested. Hypnosis was interesting. It is an altered state for some people; dreams are interesting. Could I use hypnosis to affect what went on in nighttime dreams?

Mishlove: In other words, using one altered state to influence another.

Tart: Right, and the consensus among my advisors was, "no." This experiment could not be done. Freud's idea was that day residue might affect a dream, but only in extremely indirect ways. Perhaps even many days later. But what I basically found is I could train some people to be very good at going into hypnosis. While they were in a trance state, I would suggest something specific for them to dream about that night. By specific, I mean it would have five or six unique details. Bringing them out of the hypnosis with amnesia was done so intentionally. This avoided worrying about what they were to dream about. Then they slept in my sleep laboratory. I could wake them at the end of each dream. An amazing degree of control was possible. Almost every dream would show most of the elements I suggested, in various creative forms. That was very interesting.

Mishlove: You were doing this research back in the 1960s.

Tart: That's right.

Mishlove: And it was an era in which researchers discovered for the first time that we have enormous possibilities with self-control, which were not acknowledged much until then. Biofeedback, for example.

Tart: Biofeedback was just being discovered and explored then.

Mishlove: Researchers were amazed to discover that one could learn to control the firing of a single neuron, or their heartbeat.

Tart: Yeah, the single neuron firing came along a little later. I thought my work on controlling dreams through hypnosis would inspire lots of work on the subject, but it was still too far out to make it.

Mishlove: Yet there are little pockets. It's often done outside of academia. For example, I know there are groups of people who get together to engage in mutual dreaming. I believe you wrote a chapter on that.

Tart: I don't usually think of it in those words. Take the example of the Senoi of Malaysia. There was a report by an anthropologist, Kilton Stewart, of an isolated tribe, in the jungles of Malaysia, that not only valued dreams, but they also learned to become more conscious in their dreams. Then deliberately control them. They would also all get together in the morning and swap dream stories. It was a way of social bonding. Well, I read that and was fascinated. I had no idea whether it was true or not. No other anthropologist had ever reported anything like it for this culture.

Mishlove: The Senoi people.

Tart: The Senoi, yeah. They were just too isolated. Their culture was almost wiped out during the Second World War as various armies tramped through the jungles. But I thought, well, if this culture could learn to do it, maybe it was another reason for practicing with hypnosis. The study inspired many similar groups, "We'll meet in the morning and talk about our dreams."

Mishlove: Whether the Senoi ever actually did.

Tart: That's right. But see, this was the interesting thing. I said, this guy may have dreamed up the whole thing. I am using dreams in the usual negative sense then. But when I was a kid, I had occasional nightmares. They were awful. I would wake up soaked in sweat, partially paralyzed, some monster had chased me in the dream. I would run off to my parents' bed often. I didn't like it. There came a point when I said, darn it—I wouldn't have said damn it as a young kid, all right, but with that intensity—these are my dreams, why is this happening? I taught myself to realize I was having a nightmare. Immediately, I would go back to sleep in the dream and take over. Either I would find the monster and say, "Hey, wait a minute. What are you chasing me for? What is going on?" Or I would find the monster and punch him in the nose. In almost no time, I stopped having nightmares. So, I knew personally you could learn a degree of dream control. So, I reasoned that the Senoi were possible. Whether they had been made up in fiction or not. I took a chance on publishing something that might be fiction, but it worked. All sorts of people tried the techniques. It worked for them.

Mishlove: I'm sure over the decades you have come to appreciate the esoteric schools and shamanistic training programs that describe detailed approaches to working with dreams.

Tart: Yes, Tibetan yoga techniques, for instance. Some involve a lot of work in trying to control your dreams. It's interesting because it fits in with the whole idea that part of the path to liberation is learning to regard ordinary reality as just an illusion. More like a dream manifestation, which can become tricky in terms of consequences. But yeah, so then learning to control your dreams would be a demonstration.

Mishlove: It seems you were writing in 1969 what is indicative of how we, in the West, were just catching up to advanced knowledge That maintained in Eastern esoteric traditions for centuries, maybe millennia.

Tart: And I think the key word is "starting to catch up." I think in most ways we are still just starting. We're opening to the possibility. We have explored a little here and there, but we do not yet have detailed knowledge. So, for instance, I could casually describe Tibetan dream yoga in one or two sentences. I know there are deep aspects I don't even begin to understand, much less able to describe. Or able to practice myself. I've had a few of these lucid dreams where within a dream your consciousness suddenly clears up. You know you are dreaming but you feel your consciousness as it is normally.

Now, when I tried to teach this, especially in my altered states class, I'd get some skeptics, "How do you know that you are dreaming?" And I'd say, okay, we can have a philosophical discussion. Perhaps right now you are dreaming about being in a class. You've done that a lot in real life. It would be an easy sort of dream. Are you willing to bet me 50 bucks that you can wake up in your bed, at home, in a couple of minutes? No one was interested in the bet. You can assess your consciousness and decide, this does not feel like dreaming.

The same sort of thing happens in lucid dreaming. A person may think "Gee, I know I'm dreaming. I know who I am. I know it is a dream. I can think logically. I can begin to do different sorts of things." There was some interesting clinical work on the subject initially. Psychological problems were dealt with in a much more direct way through the subconscious instead of trying to deal with them in an indirect manner. I do not think the subject has been adequately investigated and the possibilities are quite enormous.

Mishlove: You coined the phrase state-specific research.

Tart: I think I did, yeah.

Mishlove: You made it famous by publishing this new term through *Science* magazine in 1973.

Tart: It was a proposal to create state-specific sciences.

Mishlove: Lucid dreaming, could be an archetypal state-specific science. People can be trained to go into lucid dreams. We do not know yet what realms of consciousness or hyperspace are there to be explored.

Tart: Yes, exactly. My proposal basically was that ordinary consciousness, God bless it, is wonderful in all sorts of ways and totally nuts in others. It is a specialized sort of thing though and assuming it's the best possible way to think and understand is kind of silly. If the only tool you have is a hammer, must you investigate everything by hammering on it? That won't work very well for some things. So, I thought of some drug intoxication states that don't wipe out your understanding. Drugs you'd enjoy where an investigation would work, like marijuana intoxication, for instance. Lucid dreams would certainly work right there in the dream. You could say, okay, I want to investigate certain things.

For instance, Stephen LaBerge, who was a prominent investigator with lucid dreams, said, what happens if you hold your breath in a lucid dream? He had some lucid dreams in a laboratory where his breathing was being measured. Yeah, if you hold your breath in a lucid dream, your actual breathing slows down. Interesting because it might mean that communication is possible while having a lucid dream, by deliberately changing your physiology.

This is interesting too because sleep talking is relatively rare for most people. If you could train someone to sleep talk in a lucid dream, you could get on the spot descriptions. Quite interesting to find out about. I did some preliminary research suggesting this would be a possibility. Unfortunately, I didn't have enough research support to push it all the way. I had an idea I could train people to receive sound stimuli from outside: the experimenter talking to the subject in a lucid dream state, then being able to sleep talk back. It is like being able to talk to an astronaut over a radio link. We never quite got that far because again, the research support ran out, but it was fascinating work.

Mishlove: And maybe this culture hasn't quite come around to support it.

Tart: A lot of people thought this was an incredibly nutty idea. When you mentioned my proposal for state-specific sciences, it was published in *Science*, which was one of the top ten leading scientific journals in the world. It amazed me that they accepted it for publication. They sent it to two referees, one of whom clearly had no idea what it was all about and didn't say anything relevant, but the other one said it's a great idea. So, they published it.

But then the reaction was wonderful. Most scientific articles never stimulate a letter to the editor. Most scientific articles contribute little bricks of knowledge. Generally, they don't get much excitement. *Science* received over 100 letters to the editor on this paper. About half said, "You were insane to publish this article. Our ordinary state of consciousness is the only state you could possibly do science in. Every other state is psychopathological and dumb. Why were you so crazy?" And the other half said, "Hey, this is an interesting idea. Let's do it."

Now, they only published three of the letters due to space limitations. What was interesting is they sent all the letters to me. I recognized many names of quite prominent scientists. Others, I didn't know how prominent they were, but if they had a title like professor, I knew they were establishment compared to an assistant professor. And the breakdown was very interesting. The ones who said this was crazy were the well-known scientists, holding advanced academic posts, many of whom made their career in normal consciousness studies and did not like the idea of anything weird. It was the young folks who said, "Oh, let's check it out and see what we can do."

Mishlove: I should mention the movie *Altered States* picked up on your idea. I have another clip from the movie I want to show. William Hurt, the Academy Award winning actor, plays a professor talking about yoga as a state-specific technology, in service of an *a priori* hypothesis.

–Clip from the film Altered States–

Actor William Hurt: As a matter of fact, Eduardo, my year in India was disappointing. No matter how you slice it, yoga is still a state-specific technology operating in the service of an *a priori* belief system.

Actor playing Arthur: We scientists have a moral obligation to the public.

–End of Clip–

Tart: Right on. More power to them. It's going to happen eventually. Science will keep progressing. We've got to realize our tools are specialized. For example, I always carry a tool with me because it is just so handy. It's the big Swiss army knife.

Mishlove: Look at that.

Tart: And it's very handy for some things. If I need a screwdriver and a can opener, or a small screwdriver, I've got it. But I can't solve all the world's problems with a screwdriver. If I need a knife blade, I've got a knife blade. Knowing your state of consciousness is a specialized tool. This means you can then say, what is it good at doing? And I can employ it there. And what is it not good at doing? Instead of thinking there is only one way to use it.

Mishlove: And we are all capable of experiencing multiple states of consciousness.

Tart: I think everybody dreams. There are some who claim they have never dreamed. But we know the brainwave state in which dreaming is reported happens to everybody, even most mammals. So, we assume these are people who never remember dreams. And in fact, if you survey for those who claim they never dream, have them put a notebook beside their bed at night. Then ask them to write down anything they remember. Suddenly, half of them become dream recallers. They haven't turned their attention to the dreams as they are not given much value.

Mishlove: Freud, as I recall, said a dream uninterpreted is like a letter unopened.

Tart: The trouble with that analogy today is—we all get so much spam and advertising, there are many messages we don't want to open.

Mishlove: And I feel that way myself. I don't want to bother with all my dreams. We have a mutual friend, Patricia Garfield. She has written her dreams down for half a century in a journal. It has all her dreams. It's fascinating, but that task is not for everybody.

Tart: Yeah. There was a time, for instance, when I recorded my dreams. I learned some things about my psychology from it. But I think I kind of got the basic message. I don't remember my own dreams anymore. I used to have an occasional lucid dream, so I knew lucid dreams were possible. Again, that's why I published that article on the Senoi and their dream techniques. A lot of altered states I have never experienced, but according to people I respect, there are other altered states. For instance, out-of-the-body experiences. I've never experienced leaving my body while in full normal consciousness. I've talked to a few people who are perfectly honest, as far as I know, and they tell me, "This is crazy, but the other night I found myself floating to the ceiling. I was wide awake, and I could see my body on the bed." Okay, that is an interesting dream to investigate.

Mishlove: In fact, you are the person who introduced the phrase 'out-of-body experience' into the research literature.

Tart: Although, unfortunately, I originally thought out-of-the-body experiences needed an acronym to be scientific: so O-O-B-E's, out-of-body experiences. I made a terrible mistake because people started coming up to me after lectures saying, "I want to tell you about my OOBEs." I never thought anybody would pronounce it. So just OBE's, out-of-body experiences.

This is also an example of the importance of altered states. People who have an out-of-the-body experience almost always end up saying something like, "I don't *believe* my mind is going to survive death. I *know* it. I've been out of my body with my mind still functioning." This is a tremendous shift in the way they view the world; whether they'll take chances; how they want to live their life, because it's not just a belief anymore. It has become a real, personal experience. Even if the occurrence is not factually true, wow, what an incredibly powerful psychological thing to study.

Mishlove: But your research shows there are verifiable examples of clairvoyance associated with the out-of-body experience.

Tart: Yes. I was very lucky to find a person. She started talking about out-of-the body experiences when she realized I was a safe person to talk to. And she asked, "It seems very real to me. I'm floating up near the ceiling, but it can't be real, can it? It must be just a dream." And I said, "Well, take ten sheets of paper, write the numbers 1 to 10 on them. Then shuffle them in a box face down. Once you're in bed, without looking, put one on the table. If you happen to float near the ceiling that night, memorize the number." I saw her a few weeks later and she said she'd done it eight or ten times. She was always right about the number. I thought, was there anything else interesting we could research? She was moving across the country then. Luckily, I was able to have her spend several nights in my sleep laboratory. I put a five-digit number up on a shelf, then told her, if you get up there, memorize it. She reported several out-of-the-body experiences in the sleep lab but with kind of poor control and yet with an interesting brainwave state. But on the one occasion when she said she could read the number, she correctly said, oh, it's 25132. That's odds of 100,000 to one, to guess a five-digit number. So, I demonstrated that you could take an exotic, altered state, such as an out-of-the-body experience, and study it in the laboratory. And she was not near death, okay? It was a safe thing to do. Today many scientists research this subject, but I was ahead of the curve then.

Mishlove: But you did repeat that study with the famous out of body experiencer, Robert Monroe.

Tart: Yes. And he couldn't quite do as well on some things and his physiology was different. Again, it demonstrated the validity of this stuff. We can apply science and learn more about OBEs. It's not just, well, there are these weird people who have funny experiences. The idea of the soul has clearly come through an out-of-the-body experience all through history. It's not Greek theologians debating about a word that means wind and then just arrive at the concept of the soul.

Mishlove: Dr. Charles Tart, thank you so much for being with me. This has been fascinating.

Tart: In the body, as it were, but out of my mind.

13

Transpersonal Psychology

~

Recorded on November 10, 2016

Jeffrey Mishlove: Hello and welcome. I'm Jeffrey Mishlove. Today we'll be exploring transpersonal psychology. With me is Professor Charles Tart, who is one of the pioneers in the field.

Welcome, Charley. It's a pleasure to be with you once again. You were one of the early people in the transpersonal psychology movement. As I recall, the Association for Transpersonal Psychology only came into existence around 1970.

Charles Tart: Right.

Mishlove: Let's talk about what the word transpersonal means.

Tart: Well, it means *trans* in the sense of beyond, not trance like an altered state. Sometimes people have what we could loosely call mystical experiences where instead of being caught in their usual everyday identity, "I'm Charles Tart. I'm inside this body. My social security number is something that scammers would like to get," etc. They feel part of something much greater than themselves. It's not in the sense of belonging to a political organization or something, but being an intimate living part of something greater, sometimes as great as the whole universe or whatever God would be if God was the whole universe. It is expansive, which is an understatement, a life-changing experience of that sort. Ordinary psychology was totally ignorant of this kind of experience and put it down to a weird psychopathology instead of recognizing how valuable it is.

Mishlove: As I recall, the founders of the Association for Transpersonal Psychology were also the same people who founded the Association for Humanistic Psychology.

Tart: Yes, very much so.

Mishlove: People like Abraham Maslow.

Tart: The difference I usually draw between humanistic and transpersonal, which is an oversimplification, is humanists think that mainstream psychology focuses on behaviorism and psychopathology, ignoring that human beings have a lot of positive qualities such as creativity, love, and inspiration. They wanted those added to psychology, which was very important. But humanists didn't question the materialistic framework that consciousness is generated by the brain and limited by the physical laws. They were far enough out, bringing in things like love and creativity without taking on any spiritual realities.

Transpersonal psychology went a step further, including the stuff that humanists did, but said the people who have spiritual experiences say there's a reality to them and they should be taken just as seriously. Not that there isn't delusion and craziness and imagination. But we should look at these experiences seriously because they're important to people.

Mishlove: In your anthology, *Transpersonal Psychologies*, you draw on various spiritual traditions, Buddhism, Sufism, and so on, and you're analyzing them in terms of what they say about human psychology.

Tart: Yes. Over the years, I had become very involved in several different kinds of spiritual paths and knew people on other spiritual paths. There were many occasions when I thought these yogis and Buddhists had some weird ideas. Yet it kept nagging me that they seemed to be intelligent, sensible people with just some isolated weird ideas. It gradually dawned on me that maybe my cultural conditioning narrowed me down to a very tight view of the universe. Here are intelligent people who assume the universe is a certain way and within those frameworks, they're intelligent, logical, sensible people. Wouldn't it be interesting to understand from their points of view?

I realized there's a psychology within every one of those belief systems. There's a Buddhist psychology, a Sufi psychology, a Christian psychology, and so forth. But mainstream psychology couldn't see that because they weren't using the same language, the same assumptions, and so forth. So, I got the idea of getting some people who were good at a spiritual discipline to write about their discipline from a psychology perspective and treat it the way an introductory psychology book would. That's where the various contributors came in with their different kinds of transpersonal psychologies.

Mishlove: We ought to talk about the controversy that occurred. My memory is that there was an effort to set up a division of transpersonal psychology within the American Psychological Association. A very prominent humanistic and existential psychologist and a man with great respect for mysticism, Rollo May opposed it, saying it is not psychology. This is religion, and you have no business in the American Psychological Association.

Tart: As one of my psychology professors, who was rather wise, used to say to me, it's only been a hundred years since they let us out of the philosophy department, and if we don't act scientific enough, they'll send us back, and we're afraid of that. Science then was totally materialistic, so we've got to be totally materialistic. You can't consider spiritual experiences as something real but as brain pathologies, as philosophical ideas, or something. That was the kind of drive behind rejecting the division of Transpersonal Psychology.

Mishlove: The APA did, in fact, reject it. But Rollo May, who was the strongest voice, was not particularly a materialist, I don't think. He was known as an existentialist.

Tart: Well, what to say to that …

Mishlove: I interviewed him, and he spoke very highly about the influence of the German mystic Jakob Böhme on his own approach to existential psychology.

Tart: I think you can be an existential psychologist and still be a materialist. Now, I feel I'm going out on a limb saying that because I didn't study existential psychology that much. To me, they seemed too depressed and had such a grim view of life. Yes, we need to be brave and authentic, but there's a little more to it than that. From an existential position, this is the human condition to have delusions of gods, angels, divine love, and all that. We'll just have to make the best of it. I'm sure I'm distorting existential psychology terribly, though it's very good in many ways, but it's not the same as transpersonal.

Mishlove: It's generally considered a branch of humanistic psychology.

Tart: In transpersonal psychology, if someone tells me, "I left my body the other night, and it seemed perfectly clear, I was wide awake, I could see my body on the bed, and then I came back to my body," as a transpersonal psychologist, I'll say, "Oh, that's interesting. Can you give me any more details?" Everything I've been taught about science says people don't leave their bodies, but how do I know that's been investigated? It's possible that out-of-body experience is real. As a psychiatrist, I might say this person is suffering from a bad case of dissociation disorder. But a transpersonal psychologist recognizes sometimes something real may be happening. Let's find out what that reality is first.

Mishlove: Do you think there's a clear differentiation between, let's say, a spiritual teacher or guru and a transpersonal psychologist?

Tart: Yes. Very much so. A spiritual teacher, in almost all cases, knows *the* truth and is teaching that. The spiritual teacher's job, then, is to help you realign your mind so that the way you think is the way you begin to experience. But you're not being encouraged to consider multiple viewpoints. The spiritual teacher generally has a particular brand to sell, which can be extremely valuable. I'm not putting that down because a lot of people are unhappy, and if they should get involved in any spiritual training, it may make their lives much happier.

The job of the transpersonal psychologist, if they're counseling someone, is to simply ask about the troubles they're having with their spiritual tradition and to see if there are things that would help. But the job of the transpersonal psychologist as a researcher is to compare the spiritual traditions against psychological and physiological knowledge and try to find out what could be real.

Mishlove: I know one of your interests is the idea that certain spiritual disciplines are appropriate for certain personality types and not for other personality types.

Tart: My impression is that spiritual training is remarkably inefficient and ineffective. I was having a discussion several years ago with my friend Shinzen Young, who I think is one of the best meditation teachers in the world who has adapted spiritual training to fit in with the modern psyche. I asked him, "How successful are people when you teach them meditation?" He said quite casually, "If I teach a retreat or a class, just about everybody says, 'this meditation is good stuff, it's going to be a regular part of my life'." If a year later, 5% of those people are still doing it, it's successful. I was shocked. If I founded a university and 95% of my students dropped out or flunked within the first year, I'd figure we didn't know how to teach. Some students may not belong there, and there are other reasons for other students, but that's an enormously inefficient rate. I said, "Is that just your experience?" He said, "No, it's the experience of all the Western meditation teachers I know." The same thing is true of the Eastern gurus, but they don't worry about it because they all believe in reincarnation. If you drop out after a little bit, it's because you don't have good enough karma to stick with it. Maybe ten lifetimes down the road, you'll come back and train better. That might be true, but what a defense mechanism to not look at the fact that you can't teach effectively.

Mishlove: You're assuming that effective teaching means that they stick with a practice.

Tart: And that they eventually change in desirable ways. It may be crude, but it's easily measurable.

Mishlove: Spiritual disciplines typically are considered lifetime disciplines. But I can imagine that they might also have short-term applications. I'll give you an example. A dear friend of mine was experiencing spontaneous kundalini rising symptoms, having very uncomfortable shivers and energy running up and down the spine. She went to a yoga ashram for two weeks and met with the guru there, who explained what was going on and made some adjustments, and the symptoms went away. She was given a lifetime practice to follow, but as far as she was concerned, her problem was alleviated, and she was moving on to other things.

Tart: I have had many communications over the years from people who are freaking out over a spiritual or psychic thing happening to them. Making it go away is what the person wants, and that's fine. I've helped people that way a lot of times simply by saying that they aren't going crazy, I know something about this, and there's a name for this kind of phenomenon. I'm the first authority figure who's ever said anything positive to them about it, and that's all some people need.

But for the people who want to get somewhere on a spiritual path and who work at it but don't seem to get anywhere and get discouraged and quit, we need some way of knowing what discipline works well for them. I think we could help people spiritually advance a lot faster which is one of the jobs of transpersonal psychology, to start figuring that out, even if it's only approximate. If 10% stays instead of 5%, that's a big boost.

Mishlove: I suppose it would be. It does raise the issue, when we begin to talk about kundalini symptoms, of the relationship between what is known as spiritual emergencies and psychosis.

Tart: There's a model by psychiatrist Jan Ehrenwald, who was interested in parapsychology, about why people have psychic experiences. He theorized there were two basic reasons for it to happen. One he called a "need model." You *need* to know what's happening to a distant loved one, and somehow that breaks through. The need allows you to overcome the barriers against this. But the other is a "fault model." The mental filters aren't working right, information comes through, and you don't know how to handle that information. You're freaked out by it, and it can cause a lot of disturbance. Sometimes the best spiritual help to give a person is to shut the stuff down for the time being.

I had some emails a few years ago from a young woman in graduate school for one of the sciences. All sorts of psychic stuff were happening to her, and she was freaked out by it. She had gone into a scientific field thinking it would go away, because certainly this stuff doesn't happen to scientists, does it? I corresponded with her for a while, saying, "If you're into science, science starts with observation. Why don't you start taking some notes on what happens? Maybe you can look for some patterns to see if there's something there, and then what makes it decrease or increase so you're more comfortable with it." She's become one of the first of what I hope will be a whole new class of scientifically trained people who have spiritual and psychic experiences, so they can get both the inside and outside perspectives on these phenomena. She's looking for a publisher for her book now.

Mishlove: Another area where I think transpersonal psychology can be quite useful is in exploring and gaining a deeper understanding of the pitfalls that occur when you're on a spiritual path.

Tart: I had a little insight into this once though it isn't very sophisticated psychology. Years ago, I saw the original movie *The Ten Commandments*. When Moses got pissed off, he threw the tablets down, and God started destroying all those bad people I realized that I don't like when people have been mean to me, and I'd like to become more saint-like so I can destroy them, too. Maybe that's not the best spiritual motivation, but at least I know about it now and can stop kidding myself about that.

Mishlove: There are certainly conventional religions, and I can speak, having grown up in the Jewish faith, where there are many prayers saying, "God, wreak havoc on our enemies."

Tart: A lot of religion was developed basically to find a tough supernatural being who could wreak havoc on enemies. I think that's a very primitive level of religion, but I quite understand it. If I was being picked on, I'd like to have some big tough folks on my side too. But there's more to it than that, fortunately.

Mishlove: It raises an issue, and certainly one I've had to deal with in some of my own parapsychology work, coming across people who have a certain degree of psychokinetic ability along with a bad temper. What if they get angry at you and zap you somehow psychokinetically? How do you protect yourself?

Tart: My implicit prayer is that I don't meet people like that. I read your book *The PK Man* about your experiences with Ted Owens and I thought it was quite scary. I'd like to believe, as some New Age traditions say, that psychic ability can only be used for good. I don't know anything else in this world that can only be used for good. I hope it's true. I'm not going to do any experiments to find out how it can be used for bad ends. I'm more interested in the psychic and spiritual stuff that leads people to unity experiences where they're one with all life and treat every other life decently. I think that would make for a much better world.

Mishlove: I suppose it would, but if you look at the world of nature, every creature is feeding on some other creature.

Tart: I've had many discussions about this with my cat. I say that I love it when I rub it and it purrs. I know that if I were a mouse, the situation would be very, very different, and I don't get it. If I survive death and get a chance to talk with God, I'd like to find out why in the world is it like that. I must admit my great limitations here.

Mishlove: We're dealing with profound philosophical issues—the nature of evil, for example—and it does seem to me that transpersonal psychology has some things to say to address these issues.

Tart: I've avoided that part. I don't have any good ideas for dealing with evil except to help people experience the good more deeply. This comes back to my criticism of the conventional religious upbringing I had. I was told repeatedly that I *should* be good, and I *had* to be good or else, but there was very little instruction on how to be good, so I often felt bad because I was failing. I wasn't a very bad person. I'm a real low-level sinner as things go. But I worried about it because I wanted to be good. So, when I talk about spiritual paths, I usually talk about the transpersonal experiences behind religions. Somebody has one of these fantastic one-with-the-universe experiences and then talks about it, and it touches and affects people. I'd like to know how more people can have at least a taste of that so they have a real feeling, not just an intellectual conviction, that compassion, love, and wisdom are the direction we need to go.

Mishlove: We certainly can learn a lot from traditions like Buddhism. But, in mainstream Western psychology, we have Jungian archetypal psychology. I'm under the impression that Jungian psychology sits squarely in the center of the transpersonal psychology movement, wouldn't you say?

Tart: I would have said that 40 years ago. When I started getting interested in the transpersonal aspects of things, Jung was the only psychologist who was writing about it in any depth at the time, and I was very interested in his approach. But I think Jung is minor in contemporary mainstream Western psychology now. That's just how it is. He was a very smart man. Some of his ideas are good, but some of them are incomprehensible.

Mishlove: I guess I have a very different picture of Jung. I think of him as one of the great geniuses of the 20th century right up there with Freud and Einstein.

Tart: I'll agree with that, but he's not central to it. In our courses on transpersonal psychology at the Institute of Transpersonal Psychology, for instance, we might have had one course out of the whole curriculum devoted primarily to Jung, and he'd certainly be mentioned here and there, but there's enough to transpersonal psychology that nothing depends on just one writer.

Mishlove: Actually, it's a vast field if you consider martial arts, yoga, meditative, monastic, and heartfelt spirituality traditions. Bringing all of those within a psychological umbrella is an enormous task.

Tart: As an example of what seems like a contradiction, the martial art of Aikido—I spent several years getting the basics down—was created by this Japanese man, Morihei Ueshiba. When he was a child, he watched his father being beaten up by the village toughs who worked for the landlord, and he realized there's a lot of aggression in life. He learned a lot of real serious kill-somebody-else martial arts, but he was also very spiritually inclined. Eventually, he had a profound transpersonal experience in which he knew, in the depths of his being, that love and harmony are the most central forces in the universe, but a lot of people are out of harmony, and they hurt other people. So, he modified all the martial arts stuff he'd learned to an adequate defense against attacks but from a position of understanding, love, and compassion rather than, "He attacks me, I'll kick him in the stomach till he dies."

It turned into a form of transpersonal training, too. Eventually, it became a form of mindfulness training for me. For instance, when I was out on the mat working with my partner, I got into these fantasies of being a hot-stuff martial artist, but my technique was clearly awkward. When I remembered that my goal was to be present moment by moment, to sense the energy, and to blend with it, my technique got much better.

Aikido came up in my more formal work. After I had given a lecture, a fella came up and told me he'd heard several of my lectures, and he admired my technique for handling hostility. I didn't know what he was talking about. What technique? Do I have a technique? But I thought about it, and I realized Aikido helped with verbal attacks like that. I'd learned to stay centered, sense the quality of the energy coming in, and remember this is another human being who's upset, has a real concern, and he's just as valuable to the cosmos as me. How can I blend with that in a gentle manner and redirect it so there'd be some resolution rather than being the authority figure and telling them they don't know what they're talking about? It makes a difference to me. It's not that I'm all that good at it and can do it all the time, but to know that there are some ways of handling conflict that acknowledge the spiritual, and the transpersonal, is important.

Mishlove: There is a great deal that Western psychology can learn from these Eastern disciplines.

Tart: Yes.

Mishlove: Dr. Charles Tart, this has been an enlightening interview. Thank you for being with me.

Tart: Thank you for giving me the chance.

Mishlove: It's been my pleasure. And thank you for being with us.

14

How to Meditate

~

Recorded on November 10, 2016

Jeffrey Mishlove: Hello and welcome. I'm Jeffrey Mishlove. Today, we will explore how to meditate. Professor Charles Tart is an emeritus professor of psychology at the University of California at Davis and emeritus professor with the Institute of Transpersonal Psychology. Dr. Tart is an old friend, a mentor, and a former faculty member of mine. He is the author of numerous books on consciousness and parapsychology and spirituality. These include the classic anthologies, *Altered States of Consciousness*, and *Transpersonal Psychology*. He has a book of meditation called *Mind Science: Meditation Training for Practical People*. His other titles include *Waking Up* and *Learning to Use Extrasensory Perception*. Welcome, Charley.

Charles Tart: Oh, it's good to be here, Jeff. It's going to be interesting. I think of myself primarily as a scientist who in some strange way has become a kind of meditation and mindfulness teacher. But that's going to be interesting, too.

Mishlove: It will be. Your background with meditation was always difficult.

Tart: I had given up attempting to learn to meditate sometime in my 30s. It was clear it took some special talent that I didn't have. So, there was no point in even continuing to try. Fortunately, I didn't quite give up. But I think many may have this same experience.

Mishlove: I remember the first time I tried to meditate. I was expecting something special to happen. Nothing special happened at all. I've come to realize that is just fine. Something special does not have to happen.

Tart: Oh, that's advanced. It is. Oh, yes, there were many attempts at meditation. I'd sit there and think, "Gee, it's been ten minutes now and God hasn't stopped by to chat yet. What am I doing wrong?" Well, meditation. I'm going to talk about meditation in the broader context of mindfulness. Mindfulness, both in a clearer perception of what's going on, moment-by-moment, and mindfulness in understanding how your own mind is reacting and how it works.

Mishlove: Mindfulness has become a real buzzword these days. I know many people use it and use it very differently. I am glad you defined it. It's also associated with a particular type of meditation called Vipassana. And I believe it is one of the schools of meditation you studied.

Tart: I didn't define what I meant yet, though. The basic problem is both the words meditation and mindfulness are used in a wide variety of ways. And almost as if they are synonyms. Remember when people talked about consciousness raising, which in my naive way I thought meant understanding your mind better. I realized it practically meant: "When you come around to see things the way I do, you've had your consciousness raised." It's the politics of persuasion, but not what I want to talk about.

In a sense, what I am describing is dissatisfaction. If your life is going, in some sense—I've included about everybody—but if you think your life is unsatisfactory, some of the problems may come from treating your life unskillfully. You're not clear enough about what is happening. You do the wrong thing. You have automatic habits of thinking and feeling that mislead you. Then, some kind of mindfulness or meditation training can be helpful.

Mishlove: So that you break out of the cycle.

Tart: Yes. You can also get very interested in meditation and mindfulness training just out of curiosity. Buddhism talks about life as suffering. Yes, there is a lot of suffering. Yet sometimes life is nice. Even so, I've always been curious about, why am I thinking that? Why did I say that stupid thing? Why did I do so well on the task when I don't think I know how to do it, actually? Curiosity is also another good reason to want to train your mind.

I'd say the first step in learning meditation and mindfulness is getting a clearer idea of why. Why do you care? How much do you care? If you think, "maybe in five minutes I can become God," good luck. I don't think it will work. If you are curious enough or driven enough by trying to improve your life, then you must be willing to put a substantial amount of time in it. Then learn from your mistakes, because you'll make lots of mistakes. It is part of the learning process. That's when interesting things can happen.

Let's consider mind meditation: in a formal sense it usually means you will be sitting still—there are moving meditations, but for most of them you sit still. You do not react to every itch. Though you realize there will be times when if you don't scratch that itch, you are going to die. Intellectually, you know no one has ever died of not scratching an itch, but you just know you're going to die. You must learn to deal with some of that.

It's going to involve sitting still and not reacting in a usual way. Often, we react instantly to everything that happens, every sensation. We don't like it, we scratch it. Sitting still is part of the discipline. It gives you more energy to focus on your mind. When you are scratching each itch, you think, this will be the last one. I won't itch after this. But feed one itch and they all grow.

So, you sit still and remind yourself of your aim. Why am I sitting still in a quiet place? What is the point? In a sense, you refresh your worldview. What do I want out of this? It does not have to include a long, complex, intellectual analysis of everything that might affect your life. It is enough to say, OK, today I'd like to learn—how to make my mind more peaceful. Today, I would like to learn how to let experience flow through me—more easily without my interference. I don't like that— Or, ooh, more of this kind of thing.

Mishlove: You're saying you need a goal.

Tart: There are some advanced meditations which involve no goal at all, but let's not go there yet. I'm a kindergarten meditation teacher. For people who are serious and want to go a long spiritual way, they need profound meditation teachers. But I'm a very good kindergarten meditation teacher. I will get you started.

Mishlove: Well, kindergarten is the best, I think.

Tart: Yeah, and if you have a bad kindergarten experience, it's hard to do the rest. Now, a lot of people will say you can't just sit there. You must sit in a special position. We all recognize the stereotypical cross-legged position. If you are flexible enough to sit in the full lotus cross-legged posture, wow. Are you a gymnast in your daytime job, or something like that? The people who sit in the lotus posture usually start out in cultures where everybody sits on the floor, cross-legged. The body kind of shapes itself to be relatively comfortable doing that. But we are chair sitters.

Most meditation teachers would recommend you sit upright. You're not so comfortable that you can easily fall asleep, no lounge chairs. But not so uncomfortable that all you can do is grit your teeth and not do anything else. So, use a chair or similar that lets you sit still, upright, and able to focus on your internal processes. It's a good idea to decide ahead of time that you're going to meditate for a certain number of minutes. You should set a timer. Otherwise, you may sit there: "I wonder how many more minutes I have to go. Oh, it must have been 10 minutes already," or something like that. Set a timer. When I first started meditation practices, we used these kinds of parking meter timers. They would go up to an hour. Very handy. Now, sure, today there are electronic timers. In fact, there are even electronic timers which will sound nice bells.

Mishlove: Is there a minimum or maximum length of time you work with?

Tart: No. There are times when I sit down to meditate when my mind is so crazy that within a minute I say, this is ridiculous. Then I go do something more useful. Unless I'm concerned with learning to control my mental state more, in which case I might stick it out for a longer period. But—five minutes or 15 minutes—I don't think there is any sacred scripture which specifies the time.

Mishlove: TM [Transcendental Meditation] became very popular because it was 20 minutes, twice a day.

Tart: Yes. Having a specified time like that instead of having to decide each time relaxes you some. It takes a little bit of stress off, "How long should I do it?" So that's all right. Then what are you going to do? In formal meditation, there are two outstanding goals. You will find them in meditation systems all over the world. One is to learn to calm and rest your mind. The other is to gain insight into the way your mind works. If you want to learn something about calming your mind, focus on your breath. There is no pattern of how you should breathe. Just notice how you are breathing. Some people focus on the movement of your belly. Some will focus on the little sensations of the air going in and out of your nostrils. But what you don't want to do is, "Yeah, I got the nostrils thing. And there is an interesting sensation in my ear. Maybe I'll focus on that for a while. Oh, but I should be focusing on my belly." You must pick a goal and rest your attention on it.

Mishlove: You don't want to jump around.

Tart: You don't want to jump around. You don't want to strain, generally. There are some meditation forms that involve straining. Everything I say can have contradictions. But generally, it's as if I want to look at this piece of sculpture here and take it in. I put my eyes on it. I assume it is an eyes-open meditation. If I close my eyes, I will open them again only to bring it back in focus. I don't sit there philosophizing about it. Or, oh, this sculpture reminds me of a stone I saw on the beach somewhere. Blah, blah, blah, blah. You will do that all the time, of course, because our minds jump around.

Mishlove: It's going to happen.

Tart: In fact, one of the most common reactions to learning meditation is, "This is awful. It makes my mind race." It does not make your mind race. Your mind races all the time. You just finally slowed down enough to notice it. You may not like it, at all.

Mishlove: Well, you mentioned the eyes can be open.

Tart: Some meditation forms encourage eyes open. Some suggest closed. Some say adjust to your state of mind. I prefer eyes-closed meditation. But if I'm sleepy, it is a good idea to keep my eyes partly open. The light coming in makes me a little more awake. On the other hand, if my mind is very jumpy and agitated, closing my eyes generally calms me, a little, almost immediately. But if you're blinking open and closed every five seconds, you need more calmness. Do it short to begin with. Try it for five minutes. Incidentally, I have more detailed information on this subject in the webinar I teach on this subject. But I'm trying to give a general picture here.

Mishlove: Let's suppose I'm sitting down. I am about to meditate. I want to focus on my breathing, but I discover my mind is racing.

Tart: Yep. Very likely.

Mishlove: What do I do then?

Tart: Focus on your breath. Then you discover you've forgotten all about your breath and your mind is still racing. Focus on your breath.

Mishlove: You keep coming back to the central focus.

Tart: I like to emphasize, *gently* come back. It's not like, "Damn it, mind, stop that! I'm going to hold my attention on my belly no matter what." That just produces a lot of strain and stress. You certainly won't calm your mind or rest it that way. You may have to bring it back after the first minute. You may have to bring it back after the first two seconds. But just gently bring the focus back.

Mishlove: I know there's a funny scene in, I think it's Woody Allen's movie, *Annie Hall*. He's with his guru. The guru is telling him, "Relax," and he keeps saying, "I'm trying as hard as I can to relax!"

Tart: It's persistence and keep trying that count, not tension. Now, you focused on your breath, and you notice your mind is wandering. You are thinking about something else. There is a choice you can make at this point. Except sometimes, it's not a choice; it just happens. You can say, well, I've got to understand why my mind wandered. You can now spend ten or fifteen minutes trying to figure out why your mind wandered. Was it events from your childhood that led to the wander, etc., but now you are not paying attention to your breath. The much more sensible choice, to learn concentrative meditation, is, "Oh, my mind wandered. There's my breath sensation."

Mishlove: Because if a thought comes up and then you get a chain of thoughts and you may want to follow the chain. You might think, "oh, I'm getting a creative insight." But that is not the purpose.

Tart: It's a real problem. It was one of the main problems I had. My thoughts seduced me. I am sitting there and focusing on my breath. A thought comes along. It's like a beautiful woman wandered into the room and said, "Hi, Charley. You want to come with me?" You will have lots of thoughts later, OK? Don't worry.

Mishlove: Plenty of time for thinking elsewhere.

Tart: No shortage of thinking. Whenever you notice you've wandered, gently come back. Timer goes off, you're done. Now, if you want to, you can think about all the times you've failed and feel guilty and beat up on yourself. I don't particularly advise that. Just notice, "Okay, maybe I did a little better today. Maybe I did a little worse. But I sat here for five minutes, and I didn't twitch all over. I did come back to my breath occasionally. I'm slowly learning it." You learned how to make your mind race at whatever age you are. You're not going to learn to focus in five minutes. Or how to rest your mind. You just need to practice.

Mishlove: But it's not at all uncommon, to my knowledge, while meditating that every five to ten seconds, some thought may bubble up.

Tart: Gee, they never took that long in my mind.

Mishlove: Faster even, yeah.

Tart: I used to make a note in my diary if I went for two seconds without a thought. If you can rest your mind absolutely, and deep experiences come, you need to find a serious meditation teacher. And you may then get involved in some spiritual path, probably. There are a few people who find immediate positive results, right away. But for most of us, it remains difficult.

Now, I'll sketch the other main style of meditation. It's ridiculous to try to cover it in a few minutes, but this other one doesn't involve resting your mind. Rather, you learn to gently observe your mind, while it does its thing. The rough theory behind it being, since your mind is racing, it's presumably trying to accomplish something. Maybe if you could add a little consciousness, your mind would do whatever it needs to do more efficiently. Then it may eventually get clearer.

Mishlove: In other words, you are not going to focus on your breath. You're just going to watch your thoughts.

Tart: Now, don't jump to that too fast. That will be very difficult. Usually, the way Shinzen Young showed me, which was very helpful, he said, "Notice any sensations in your body." If I was doing that now, there's a throbbing in both hands. My right leg has a little tension in the calf muscles. There is throbbing in the hands again. There's a little painful sensation in the back of my head. The way I am trying to notice them is not to grab them, and not, "Oh, I think that's a spiritual sensation. I want more of it." Nor "That's a little bit of a pain quality. I'm going to look for another sensation and make that go away somehow." You try to develop a way of observing. What is going on, with some concentration. You watch it for at least a half a second or a second. This is versus a glance and then going off focus, to your loss. Or you may begin wondering stuff. With concentration, with clarity, by slowing down slightly and looking at it with a little more concentration. thoughts will usually become clearer.

As I'm talking to you, there is a vague realization of some kind of sensations in my hands. When I turned my attention to it, they are very well-defined sensations. There's a pulse as well. Not that you need to feel your pulse, but you're observing with more clarity what's going on. You observe with equanimity. You do not grab or push away. You don't evaluate. It is what it is. That can get very interesting.

Mishlove: Is it primarily bodily sensations?

Tart: Body sensations is an easy place to start. Your body is always with you. If I say you start by observing the benevolence of God, what would I look at? That's kind of vague and abstract, [unlike] the sensations in your body. If you cannot do your whole body, if that seems too complicated, just attempt to feel what's in your left hand, or your right thumb. But you will be learning to gently keep your attention on a target, on an area. It's an area where things are changing and flowing. Do this rather than trying to fix it as: inhale, exhale, inhale, exhale. This is eventually going to lead to more insights and be more useful in everyday life, too. Where all sorts of things are flowing all the time.

If you are stressed out by a situation in life, you usually cannot say, "Stop, I need to sit still, cross-legged, and focus on my breath for five minutes before I answer your question." That's not terribly practical most of the time. But if you can focus on this stressful situation with equanimity: "Oh, OK, I'm not going to freak out. I'm not going to clap my hands. I'm going to look more clearly." This may often solve a lot of problems, then and there.

It's especially interesting with respect to pain. Shinzen expressed it very nicely in a little equation, $S = P \times R$. S is suffering. Suffering is your psychological reaction. You know what suffering is; you've been there. P, pain, is the actual physical sensation, which can vary in intensity. R is your mental resistance. You may have a little physical pain but, "Oh my god, I don't deserve it. It's not fair, and I've been meditating." You multiply pain by a lot of resistance. You can have enormous suffering from a very tiny pain. Or if you learn to let things flow with more equanimity, you may have strong physical pains and not suffer from them. It's a sensation. I'm not freaking out about it and multiplying the suffering. It's not a big deal. Now, you must develop some skill before that response is possible, of course.

Mishlove: Many years ago, courtesy of you, I interviewed Shinzen Young. He makes a point of saying, "Notice if there's an attachment or an aversion to the pain. Or even an emotion associated with it. Then realize the emotion isn't you. It is just the attachment."

Tart: Now, you have just suggested upping the level of the meditation some. At first, you just want to notice what these sensations are. Eventually, you will notice them in more detail. Like I said, if I pay attention. There was a boundedness to the sensation in my hand. Sometimes it got bigger and then smaller. A lot of body sensations can get very interesting this way.

Eventually, to develop this more easily, and not necessarily the only way, but most easily, start from the body. You may then be able to apply it to emotions. "Yes, I feel anger. That anger has several components. It is a physical tension and part of it is a fear sensation. Some come from jealousy. That's interesting." Seeing the different parts of emotion, allows one to understand better, whereas with a mixture, it has more control over you.

Mishlove: In effect, the basic meditation method you teach is not so different from old-fashioned introspection.

Tart: I don't want to equate this with old-fashioned introspection. You are looking inside. You try to understand things better. Applying these principles of concentration, clarity, and equanimity makes it different. You're also doing it within an overall context. Remember I said, find out why you want to learn meditation or mindfulness. Refresh yourself on that decision at the beginning. The overall context will have subtle effects on what you do. Introspection to report to a researcher how certain things feel is a whole different mental set than if I am trying to deeply understand.

In my webinar course and books, I teach leading individuals toward increased mindfulness in everyday life. Very few people ever get in trouble through what they feel and think while sitting on a little meditation cushion or comfortable straight-backed chair. But we get in trouble all the time. We are not very mindful of how we are feeling or what we say in real life. We ask ourselves later, "How could I have been so stupid as to say that? How thoughtless was I? No wonder she won't speak to me anymore." If you can bring more mindfulness to everyday life, it reduces suffering. It increases your ability to do something effective both for yourself and other people.

Mishlove: The suggestion there seems to be that life itself can be a meditation.

Tart: Yes. Shinzen formally defines meditation as applying the principles of concentration, clarity, and equanimity. Incidentally, I'm primarily talking with Shinzen stuff here because it is clearly understandable. There are other ways you can analyze meditation. But Shinzen is a genius with meditation adaptations. If you become good, you should find a teacher like Shinzen, not me. For beginners in mediation, I am a good kindergarten teacher.

Mishlove: You are a good introductory teacher because you're a psychologist. And you have studied with many meditation teachers along the way.

Tart: And I've had enormous difficulties in learning how to meditate. I know what that feels like. There are a few people who I find absolutely disgusting. They get two minutes of instruction and experience cosmic consciousness or similar. It's not fair. They make it seem so easy. It's like martial arts, like when I was learning Aikido. The black belt teacher would demonstrate some technique, and I didn't get it. I'd ask for an explanation and he or she would demonstrate it again. I still didn't get it because it was so natural and easy for them, at their point of mastery, they no longer recognized the difficult spots. So, I'd find some intermediate level student who had only learned to do it well recently. One who remembered the difficulties and could explain the movement better.

Mishlove: Charley Tart, thank you so much for sharing the skill of meditation. It is a very valuable practice for people.

Tart: I've just given some very basic hints to get started. I hope it motivates some people to give it a try. Meditation may introduce the individual to a general skill that could then apply to various spiritual systems.

Mishlove: Thank you for being with me.

Tart: My pleasure.

15

Future Psychenauts

~

Recorded on October 23, 2018

Jeffrey Mishlove: Hello, I'm Jeffrey Mishlove. Today we will be exploring the future and psychenauts. Psychenauts are the astronauts of inner space.

Welcome, Charley. It's a pleasure to be with you again. Today we will focus on an idea from which you achieved a certain amount of renown in 1972. Your published article in *Science* magazine on the topic of state-specific science: the idea that researchers can enter altered states of consciousness and conduct experiments from within those states.

Charles Tart: You could call it renown, or you could name it infamy. I was amazed that *Science* accepted the article for publication. I wanted them to, because I thought what I had to say was relevant to expanding science in all fields, not just psychology. They are the establishment's big journal. One of the most interesting results of that article was the over one hundred letters to the editor written. Now, normally, scientific articles get zero letters to the editor, or maybe one or two. They got a hundred responses. The people who wrote them divided roughly 50-50 between those who said, "This is preposterous! Every state of mind but our normal state is insanity. You can't possibly do science in an illogical, irrational state of mind." The other half all said, "Wow, this is right on. Let's get with it." What was even more interesting—they only published a few of these letters—but they sent them all to me. I could look at who sent them, and I recognized a lot of the names. The people who said "anything but our ordinary state is crazy" were older, established scientists. The people who said, "Let's do it," were younger scientists. So, oh my goodness, do not trust anybody over 35.

Mishlove: The interesting thing is that now we can look back on that groundbreaking article from nearly half a century of perspective.

Tart: You're making me feel old.

Mishlove: Well, now you are the old, established guy yourself.

Tart: Oh, dear. All right, careful now, Jeff.

Mishlove: I do think the article was way, way ahead of its time. You make a point of questioning whether state-specific science would be possible. You listed several objections that would make this style of research extremely difficult. Looking back, there have been a few small endeavors, but we do not yet have a department of state-specific science in any university.

Tart: No, not at all. Let me say something about what I was basically proposing. I've been interested in various altered states of consciousness for years. I did dissertation research using hypnosis, for instance, to affect nocturnal dreams. I was aware of psychedelic induced states and all that. One of the things it made clear to me was that we take our ordinary state of consciousness for granted. It is just there. It's normal. But it is a construct. It's some outcome of whatever we are biologically given plus culture. Social mores teach you how to see and think. It's like, oh, for instance, your culture teaches you to look at everything through this kind of lens [holding a magnifying lens]. This has great advantages. Things you might otherwise miss appear because they're bigger. Yet at the same time, it distorts your view of the world, making it more likely you miss other things.

So, I thought, is it possible to use a state of consciousness like a tool? You apply it when it's appropriate and helpful. You stop using it and go on to employ some other state. I love the process of science because otherwise I get carried away by ideas. I want to be able to do research in several ways. Some scientists will do that. They never talk about it. The social aspect of science is that we only talk about everything that is perfectly logical. I was presented with the problem. I rationally thought about every step of it, came to this conclusion, and did this experiment. Instead of: I woke up in the middle of the night with this crazy idea. I checked it out, and then I wrote it up logically.

Mishlove: The possibility for performing research in altered states is quite large. Back in the 1970s, Timothy Leary referred to ingesting LSD as akin to becoming a microscope to your own psyche.

Tart: I think some drugs can be used that way. This is where we go back to the practical difficulties you mentioned. Most ordinary microscopes don't intoxicate you, and by that, I mean a person has a psychedelic experience. It is so incredible compared to their ordinary state. They see all sorts of new things. It feels wonderful and they are liable to get overly attached. In a way, pure science would say, "Okay, I see things this way now. Let's check it out and see what can be done," instead of: "Now I have the truth."

I thought about that in a very interesting way. I'll tell you a story. My first experience with psychedelics was in the late 1950s. This was before most people ever heard of these drugs. I met an Austrian psychologist on sabbatical at Duke University. He and I got talking. We both had an interest in parapsychology. He mentioned his recent research on mescaline. Well, I happened to have read Aldous Huxley's book on mescaline, *The Doors of Perception.* I thought it very interesting, but it was all quite intellectual, of course. He said he didn't know of any studies of Americans who had ever taken mescaline and reported on the outcomes. So, I volunteered to represent my country. It was a sacrifice because I had to skip breakfast, so I'd have an empty stomach—a real hardship for me at the time—but Huxley's book said it would be interesting. And it was all for science. So, we did it. I had an incredible experience.

But as I look back over the years, I realize how much my setting, my expectations affected what happened. I thought of it as a scientific experiment. I thought of it as at least affecting my brain so that things computed and were perceived in a different manner. So, in some ways I was able to experience some aspects of it—I don't want to say objectively, but not by getting carried away with "Oh wow! This is the best thing that ever happened. I know all the truth!" But suppose I was still very religious, like I was when I was a kid. If I had been praying for God to give me a sign, and that same experience happened, I would have felt it to be a special, mystical blessing. My thoughts of the experience, afterwards, would have been extremely different.

The way one perceives is very important. One caveat for the idea of state-specific sciences is that some will say, "I want to turn into that wonderful state where I know everything. Everything is then perfect. I become a superior enlightened being." I can then stop thinking, experimenting, or looking at alternatives. It is possible to get stuck like that. Just because you feel enlightened doesn't necessarily mean you are.

Mishlove: That would be one of the pitfalls of working with intoxicating drugs. But there are other altered states of consciousness that you have explored. Hypnosis being one that involves a mild alteration of consciousness. Yet it can be quite interesting.

Tart: There were some lines of research in the field, usually started by one or two people using hypnosis to induce something like a psychedelic state, without involving any drugs. Of course, it was much more controllable as to what parts were stressed back then. Arthur Hastings did some studies on giving people a hypnotic-like induction, people with MDMA. He found changes in the way their mind functions. Again, it goes back to the tool analogy, of which I am very, very fond. You know that I always have a Swiss army knife with me.

Mishlove: A big one.

Tart: The biggest one, right? I love it. I use it for all sorts of things, but I don't worship it. I do not think, "Now I have *the* tool that will reveal all." It's very good for some things; not very good for other things. I think we need to have that attitude toward all states of consciousness. What is this tool good for and what is it probably distorting, or misleading, or something like that? It will require a lot of discipline, if it feels good.

Mishlove: One of the points that you make in your excellent paper—I reread it just last night, and it felt in many ways very contemporary—but one of the points you made is if we look at esoteric traditions and meditative practices, they bear a resemblance to what you're describing as state-specific research. It suggests the possibility that maybe somewhere hidden in the mountains of Afghanistan there is a monastery where people practice state-specific science, for maybe centuries.

Tart: That may well be, but again there is the other side. We must remain conscious of this fact. They may be practicing state-specific indoctrination. That is, when you are being guided in an altered state by someone who knows the way. Since the state is malleable, in a way, you might have wonderful experiences. They make it clear that this point of view is *the* ultimate truth. But it is only one way of looking at things. The ability to let go and step back, as well as get into it, is essential to the use of altered states in exploring the mind.

Mishlove: Characteristic of not just the scientific method but philosophical inquiry is to question your premise.

Tart: That's right. On the other hand, in graduate school you are given certain problems. You are challenged to find the right answer. If you don't keep getting the right answers, you don't get a degree. Then you will not advance in that science. People learn to fake the right answer. Many do so creatively but it's hard to resist that indoctrination thing. We are social animals.

Mishlove: I suspect the problem of indoctrination exists as much in a normal state of consciousness as it does in any altered state.

Tart: Yes, very much so.

Mishlove: The other thing that strikes me is in various forms of dreamwork, it is very hard to confine any dream to ideology. Dreams seem to naturally transcend any logical container.

Tart: Normally, in the dreams of undisciplined people. Someone heavily trained and reinforced in a specific way of thinking and perceiving, this may shape their dreams. I don't think we have any data on how effective that is, but I certainly know in meditation that can happen. I think of basic Buddhist meditation, the Vipassana kind, as a wonderful way of exploring the mind. You learn to experience more clearly what's happening around you. Not being attached to the frustrations of, " ... if it changes to this when you'd like that." Meditation is a wonderful tool. But then again, you go into it having been taught, "There is an enlightened way you want to learn and experience". Possibly you will have a teacher saying, "Well, you should practice more on that one. This is interesting but not the right direction," and so forth. So even a very flexible tool like Vipassana meditation may be biased to distort.

Mishlove: But how different is that than walking into the psychology laboratory and having your instructor show you the best way to use a tachistoscope, for example?

Tart: There is a great deal of similarity. It keeps coming back to the fact that we are social animals. We want approval from our peers; everybody, if we can get it. One of the things meditation practices like Vipassana yield, if done right, is noticing. When you think or do because it is for social approval, that matters. Even while you tell yourself you are learning to perceive more clearly. If you can see this, it will force you to work on you. You will then have more chances of letting go.

Mishlove: The human capacity for self-deception is big.

Tart: Yeah. I thought about this concept while involved in the early hypnosis research. Maybe 15-20 percent of the population have a tremendous ability to achieve a deep hypnotic state. They are extremely responsive to suggestion. It made me think, I can temporarily mold this person's consciousness, in very powerful ways. Suppose I encouraged them to have spiritual experiences, or what I thought were spiritual experiences. I have never tried it because it struck me as extremely unethical. That is not what an experimental subject in a hypnosis study expects as an outcome. They expect to come out the same person as they went in. Many meditation techniques as compared with hypnotic techniques, boy, they sure are similar.

Mishlove: You gave a presentation a couple of months ago to the annual conference of the Parapsychological Association. You explored in some detail how psychenauts of the future could be trained in the art of out-of-body travel. Potentially, they can begin to map, using some sort of consensus methodology, what those realms may look like.

Tart: Yes, and I think there are great possibilities there. Now, I am violating conventional norms. They attempt to explain all this away. "Oh, it's just a malfunctioning of lobe number 19 in the brain," or something like that. But I think experience is data and worthy of research. What are the rules or laws governing it? What can we do with it? The experiences gathered from out-of-the-body or in various meditative states deserve study. Yeah, discovery of what they are to the brain is involved. You cannot speak without using your brain. Well, some people seem to talk without using their brain, don't they? Sorry. ...

Mishlove: That was a little digression.

Tart: Yeah, that was a little digression. So, I think that's important to do. The word you used, consensus, is critical. When Raymond Moody's book on near-death experiences came out, what was that 1970, 1971, something like that?

Mishlove: *Life After Life.*

Tart: *Life After Life*, yeah. I knew about those kinds of experiences because I read weird esoteric literature. It is writings generally unknown to the culture. But what impressed me about the book was Moody's findings. People of different religious beliefs or no religious beliefs but who come close to death have very similar qualities of experience.

If Christians saw the pearly gates and Hindus, Yama, the god of death, you'd say, "Well, this is some kind of culturally induced hallucination." But the similarity implies they are talking about something real. There are a lot of things in life [where] consensus is all we need. I've never been to Warsaw. I believe in Warsaw because I have read of or talked to people who say they have been to a place named Warsaw. They all describe it the same way. If people have been to a place, a state, they describe similarly, it is not an obvious projection of cultural biases. That gets interesting.

Mishlove: Moody and others have mapped out the idea [that] you are passing through a tunnel. There is a light at the end of the tunnel. There do seem to be commonalities across cultures, especially regarding a near-death experience. There was even a movie on the subject many years ago. I think the movie title was *Flatliners*. The idea of the movie was to induce near-death experiences similar to state-specific research.

Tart: Yeah, that is a little more extreme than I would advocate. The "near" part is very tricky.

Mishlove: It's not likely to get past the Human Subjects Committee.

Tart: And most people who come that near don't give us an interesting report. They die.

Mishlove: Yet psychology was born in the 19th century: a time when researchers, in all the labs going back to Wilhelm Wundt, used introspection as a research methodology. This method was abandoned after a decade or two when it was determined that introspection was not reliable.

Tart: Well, that's it. Different laboratories kept coming up with different results. But in retrospect, it is quite understandable why they ran into the problem. First off, they were modeling themselves on chemistry. It is one of the more glamorous sciences. What are the elements of the mind? What kind of compounds do they form and how do they react? If we understand this, we will start to understand the functioning of the mind. That's sensible. We have made progress by finding the parts and discovering how they work together.

But when you look at what was done in the first place, it was done in a very authoritarian cultural setting. Herr-Doktor-Professor, who hired you, had ideas on the sort of things that should be found. You might lose your job if you didn't come up with them. Then this Herr-Doktor-Professor didn't have quite the same view as another. They talked about [how] they were trained observers. Training then meant five to ten hours of some kind of experience. But I've talked with some meditation teachers about the Vipassana concept, on how to experience things clearly without distortion. What is adequate training? They say maybe 5,000 to 10,000 hours. We are talking about untrained observers, so it is not surprising their observations differ tremendously. It's Experimenter bias, or a whole bunch of things on why that research didn't work. You can control for those things if you know about them to some extent. If not, they run rampant in the lab.

One of my most interesting experiments goes back to my hypnosis experiment days. A big question in the scientific study of hypnosis was, is it some special altered state of consciousness that makes people more suggestible, or is it sort of a social situation? "I did the woo woo thing and now you're going to be—" So, you play the role and take the part and so forth. We did what was an obvious experiment for the time. We standardized a way of measuring how much a subject responds to a suggestion. We developed a scale of twelve items, and you basically read an item. Hold out your hand and imagine it is feeling heavy. Just think about: does the hand lower at least twelve inches by the time you complete reading this? You can score how suggestible somebody is in this way.

We ran tests on subjects under two conditions. One group went through a hypnotic induction procedure, which incidentally, it is poor to assume they were hypnotized, because a lot of people do not respond. But anyway, they went through the procedure. The other group we chatted with for ten minutes, in a social sort of way. Presumably they were not hypnotized, except we know that highly suggestible people could get hypnotized anyway. We had eight or nine different experimenters. I would run my first few subjects. After a while, I noticed that I was not treating them equally. If not hypnotized, I gave suggestions to a subject in a kind of business-like manner. "Hold out your hand and imagine a heavy object in it," and so forth. But if the hypnosis induction procedure was complete, it was more like, *"Hold out your hand and imagine a heavy object in it and what that heavy object would feel like."* There was something more seductive, sexier about my voice.

Well, wait a minute. If you give tests to subjects in different ways, you get a difference in outcome. What does this mean? It does not explain their internal state or what it might mean. This is an example of experimental bias. Psychology has still not matured enough to cope with it. It's almost a social bargain to pretend it's not there. So, a lot of what we think are solid psychological findings are probably a matter of experimenter bias. The subjects were nice. They figured out what you wanted, and they wanted science to work, so they performed as expected.

Mishlove: Not to mention the possibility of some sort of telepathic contamination.

Tart: Yes. I think that is one of the main reasons there is so much irrational opposition to parapsychology. If you surmise, uh oh, here's another channel for bias to go through. We have no idea how to turn it off. That is scary and wrecks too many tests.

Mishlove: What is your feeling about the prospects for developing state-specific research today?

Tart: I think the prospects are very good. It will require researchers devoted enough to not just fall in love with a particular altered state. They must truly want to help learn about it. That means, for instance, pre-selection of those curious instead of: "Oh, I want to get high." Not that there's anything wrong with wanting to feel wonderful and have insights and so forth. However, you want people involved to be curious about the subject and not too attached. Much like the old Buddhist prayer, you pray one can live without too much attachment or too much aversion, so they can look back in fairness. Only then can you begin to train people. Especially when trained to notice attachment, so you can say, no, the data we got here is not very good. You wanted a particular outcome too much.

Mishlove: Let me approach the subject from a different angle. I think, in the last 46 years since your paper was originally published in *Science* magazine, there have been as many as 1,000 studies of meditation using advanced meditators. Those with years of practice, such as monks and lamas and gurus, have come into the laboratory for physiological measurement.

Tart: Yeah. We have a head start. These people may be better at working without attachment. But I don't know how you physiologically measure whether someone is overly attached to a particular outcome. If we started researching that subject, we might find out. It's another characteristic we need in subjects. Those willing to admit, "I don't know." For instance, I look back at my article in *Science* sometimes and think, like you described it earlier, it was ahead of its time. It is so brilliant that the world wasn't ready for it. Oh, that feels good. Or maybe I was full of it. That is a real possibility.

Mishlove: Well, it was a bold conjecture. You outlined more than a scientific discipline; a whole new way of doing science.

Tart: I think it's important. If you can change your state of consciousness, while understanding your mind, it is a new key to happiness that does not require using global resources and heating up the planet faster. This can be accomplished without having to destroy our ecology. So, to me, it's important to help people understand this better.

But there is a lot of resistance. I'll tell you another story about the state-specific *Science* paper. Shortly after publication, I attended a conference on dream research, held on the East coast that year. Dream research was new and hot then. There were hundreds of people attending. After the conference, I flew back to California on a plane with a young psychiatrist. We got to talking about state-specific sciences and parapsychology. He didn't know anything about these subjects. I started educating him a little. By the time we were halfway across the country, the psychiatrist in the seat next to me, every 10 minutes, would turn to me saying, "Either I've been missing something, or you are crazy."

Well, okay, could be. Scientists are irrational. They try to be rational. They are very good at rationalizing in some specialized ways. We do not train researchers to be more rational or less attached. We do not train them to be creative either. We assume it will happen somehow, if they know the facts of scientific truth. That's not enough.

Mishlove: It strikes me your proposal could be viewed in two ways. On one hand, you suggest: let's take knowledge available from altered states of consciousness and bring it into the scientific community. The other approach might be the following: Let's take all the wisdom available in the scientific method and introduce it into various spiritual communities. Those already engaged in altered states practice.

Tart: That's brilliant when you put it that way. The second one may be even harder than introducing scientists to altered states. I've found most religious people I know are awfully attached to their version of THE

TRUTH, in capital letters. It's all right if science does something that fits in with their thing. They don't want to hear about science questioning part of it. Can one become objective and open and curious enough to say, "I have given my life to this tradition. There is a lot of truth here, but some parts of it may be wrong. Should we look at it?" That's tough.

Mishlove: It is tough. Over the years, I have heard many spiritual teachers say those words, exactly. They often remark, don't follow any of these tenets because I tell you. Test them for yourself. See if it works. Keep what is best for you and feel free to discard the rest. Even the Buddha said as much.

Tart: That's right. The Buddha said, in sutra number so and so, which you might be able to understand, someday, if you take the right path. There is a lot of lip service paid to this idea. I don't know how much it reflects in the actual practice of teaching. There is the interaction between a teacher and a student, in the spiritual disciplines. It is very subtle. All sorts of things can be conveyed that intellectually look like open-mindedness is being taught. Yet the person is constantly being steered in the "proper" direction.

Mishlove: You used an interesting example in the presentation you made to the Parapsychological Association. The case study of a man that you knew very well, Robert Monroe. He is the author of several books on out-of-body experience, who reported something very specific. He had numerous visits to a particular locale that he always came to in the very same way. Raising about two feet above the bed, he then pushed through a hole that opened in the wall in front of him. He visited an unusual society that he kept revisiting. It was like another planet. This dream world had certain consistencies to it [on] each visit. For example, there were vehicles that were much wider than they were long.

Tart: Yeah, which is a crazy way to design a vehicle in terms of mechanics. Otherwise, the place looked a lot like our ordinary, physical world. But you don't make cars wider than they are long. Your roads would have to be two or three times as wide. They're not as stable on the turns. Monroe was practically an engineer, so he was aware of this kind of thing. Yet it was consistent from visit to visit.

Mishlove: So, it does suggest, at least in terms of the consistency from visit to visit, that this might be a real location somewhere. Perhaps within, just for lack of a better word, I'll call it hyperspace. Some other dimension only accessible through consciousness itself. You are proposing that perhaps people could be trained to go through the exact same steps. Those Monroe went through to arrive at that location. Where they could see if they observed the very same things as Monroe, with some consistency.

Tart: Yeah, ignoring possible difficulties for a moment, it would be like using Warsaw as an example again. We take some people who do not know anything about Warsaw. We blindfold them and take them to a spot in the city. Once they arrive, the blindfold comes off and eyes are opened. We instruct: "Go wander around for an hour and come back. Then give us a report on what you see here." If everyone who did that gave you a totally different story, you would think they are hallucinating like mad when they go outside. But if they give you consistent reports, "Yeah, there is a very tall building on the left, there's a canal beside ..." you would think, oh, that is an example of something there.

So, the question then becomes: is Monroe's technique of floating in the air in his out-of-the-body body—what an awkward way of talking, but that's the way he experienced it—and feeling a wall with a hole he then goes through, is it sufficient? If you could train people, and they had no other expectations of what to experience, then describe similar experiences to Monroe's, I would start thinking it is worthwhile to think of it as a real place, in hyperspace. A place in a physical space, certainly not here.

Mishlove: Isn't that approach not so different from the 19th century approach of—He called himself Allan Kardec, the founder of the Spiritist movement. He was a French pedagogue. His actual name was Hippolyte Léon Denizard Rivail. He worked with trance mediums—I think he had seven—and waited for all seven to agree about some description of the afterlife. Only then, did he accept it. If he could get consensus from seven different mediums, he would determine an example [to be] a valid description.

Tart: That is excellent. Of course, I want to know how much these mediums knew about the afterlife to begin with. But it would be technically feasible in a sense to find people with mediumistic abilities who have never heard of spiritualism. Then raise them in an isolated way that would develop their mediumistic capacity without saying, "And such and such is the way it goes," and so forth. Then see how much agreement you get. But, of course, you raised the possibility of telepathic contagion before, which messes up everything. We cannot solve all the problems at once. I do not want to think that we can contaminate so thoroughly with telepathy that we may never discover individual reality. That's no fun.

Mishlove: It strikes me that many of the methodologies used in parapsychology could be employed in altered states. It would be interesting to learn more about the altered states that seem to favor paranormal abilities.

Tart: I think there is a general principle here. There's no experiment that would prove it. The general principle: any altered state is likely to favor paranormal abilities simply because, while in your ordinary state, you are told that stuff is impossible and crazy. Now, oh wow, the whole world is different. Maybe it can happen here, too. Whether there may be specific talents for specific altered states, I don't know.

Going back to my first psychedelic experience with mescaline, I had agreed to do a card-calling test to test my ESP. I was exploring the universe in this mescaline-induced state. They asked me to guess at cards: "Is it a star or a wave or a square …?" This was so trivial compared to what I was experiencing. The question becomes, how do you find a task to test psychic sorts of things, or employ psychic things, in a particular altered state that makes sense? I know in my own experiments, I have always tried to not run the subjects. And my co-experimenters explore particulars, so the experiment makes sense to them as well. That's no guarantee there will be no bias problem. I think it does get closer to less craziness, less bias.

Mishlove: In your book, *Altered States of Consciousness*, there was a chapter on mutual dreaming.

Tart: Mutual hypnosis.

Mishlove: Mutual hypnosis, okay. It reminded me that I did an interview about mutual dreaming, which is akin to mutual hypnosis, many years ago. A woman named Linda Lane Magallón wrote the book, *Mutual Dreaming*. She worked with groups. They would regularly meet and get to know each other. Then they would go home and dream, but with the intention to meet each other in their dreams. They would report on their dreams to the group. She said it was like being at a party. You would encounter others in your dreams. She believed they were having some success with this method.

Tart: I think that's fascinating. I vaguely recall seeing something about it. It was a long time ago, so I can't say anything in detail. In mutual hypnosis, you have more control keeping subjects focused. I was working with the idea of a special rapport between the hypnotist and a hypnotized person when in the altered state. I began working with two experimentalists, who hypnotized others, with a fair amount of hypnotic talent themselves. So, A would hypnotize B. When B was hypnotized, B would then hypnotize A. Subject A would then deepen B, and B would deepen A, and your head's going back and forth. This is hypnotic here, too. That's good.

They had a fascinating mutual experience and described it as it progressed. Some suggested there were even signs of paranormal effects. The experimenters started describing a cave environment and features of the cave—no, I'm not telling this right. Afterwards, they wrote a more detailed account than the oral references, which I recorded. They described similar features in the notes not spoken during the session. Some people wondered, well, maybe they were telepathically interacting. Maybe, I don't know. But that would certainly lead to this same sort of thing. They only talk about A, B, and C, but they both mentioned D, E, and F. Interesting.

Mishlove: This reminds me of a long-ago personal experience, when I lived in California. I was invited to be part of a group who practiced mutual hypnotic induction, combined with remote viewing.

Tart: Was that Freda Morris? I remember she was doing something with that.

Mishlove: No, this was with a chiropractor named Dr. Richard Gierak. He lived down in Walnut Creek then. So, we would be, all of us in a hypnotic trance. Somebody would say, "Oh, let's fly together." We would meet at the top of the Golden Gate Bridge, on one of the towers. Then someone might say, "Let's fly over to Marine World, USA." Another would suggest, "Yeah, let's check out the dolphins," and then "Oh, look, there's a dolphin in the tank, by itself. The dolphin is sick and alone and lonely. She wants us to rescue her. The dolphin's name is Dee, or it begins with a D. This dolphin is cantankerous and won't cooperate with the other dolphins. Isn't that strange?"

We came out of this mutual state saying, "Wait, what happened here? Let's call up Marine World and see if they have a dolphin like that." Well, it turned out they did. There was a dolphin named Dondi. The dolphin trainers were very excited. They said, "Yeah, Dondi has been separated from the other dolphins. She won't cooperate and is unhappy. We do not know what to do. Why don't you come over and meet Dondi." We did a whole process—it wasn't adequately scientific—but it was a study to see if we could give Dondi telepathic suggestions. Encouraging her to perform different tricks. It seemed to work. Dondi was—we couldn't free Dondi—but Dondi was returned eventually to the dolphin show and performed with the other dolphins after this encounter. It seems something as simple as mutual hypnotic induction can be quite powerful.

Tart: You mentioned one of the factors that makes paranormal functioning more likely. Especially If you're doing it in a group, where everybody accepts the reality of the paranormal. Again, we are social animals. We reinforce one another. I am not a nut thinking this stuff is even possible. It's the group doing it. I find these kinds of observations very interesting. It's not like the only way we can learn is from laboratory experiments. They are nice, but the lab can be awfully artificial.

Mishlove: My suspicion is there are many like Dr. Richard Gierak, the chiropractor. Others that have formed small groups, of less than a dozen people. There are probably a thousand groups out there. People at an amateur level, but still quite serious about engaging in what you term state-specific research.

Tart: They're communicating through the Internet, too. Reinforcement in this manner is something very different. I think it has very interesting possibilities. Again, I have spoken with so many in my life about their repeated paranormal experiences. And they were worried by them. They believe they must be nuts because science has proven their experiences should not happen. I must be crazy to think it happens. Just to tell these people, no, wait a minute, that has a name. It doesn't mean you are crazy. Or you might be crazy; I don't know you. I do know you cannot diagnose yourself from this type of paranormal experience. This is garden variety telepathy. Relax and enjoy it. Learn something from it.

Mishlove: When you and I started in the field, people wouldn't learn about this at all. Only if they read the books or were lucky enough to find a course in parapsychology. Today, I happen to know there are over a thousand, probably several thousand discussion groups on Facebook, LinkedIn and other social media networks. Paranormal topics and altered states of consciousness and spiritual community members now communicate openly with each other.

Tart: That's very interesting, Jeffrey. It adds to something I have been thinking about the last few days: the history of parapsychology. It's had a very hard time making it in our culture. The establishment authorities say there is nothing there. It is all a delusion. But in my lifetime, your lifetime, there have been a couple of occasions when it has almost broken through to wider acceptance. For instance, the development of the remote viewing paradigm, when various intelligence agencies began using it for information in intelligence planning. That alone provided more support for parapsychology than in probably all its previous history. Yet It couldn't quite make it beyond there. But then Russell Targ and Hal Puthoff adapted remote viewing to make money through silver futures. If you want to break into popular culture with psi, show them a way to make money from it.

The Internet connecting people together through reinforcements may be a third attempt. We might be getting enough critical mass that the culture will think more openly and positively about parapsychology. I think this is important. Ask yourself, what are we human beings? The establishment view, although it never likes to put it so boldly, is we are a chemical accident. We don't mean a damn thing. If I manipulate you and you feel pain, so what? That's not my nervous system and I make a profit. Big deal. You are just a chemical reaction. This view permeates so much of modern life. It is very depressing at some level.

We have spiritual traditions and religious traditions that tell us, "Yeah, sure, there's a lot of chemistry going on here, but there is something more; something bigger; something meaningful." We need some demonstrations to reach a lot of people. For those who have religious faith, they don't have a problem. There are probably fewer nowadays with this pervasive negative atmosphere. But if they realize, well, wait a minute, prayer; prayer is talking to yourself, right? It's a waste of your breath. Wait a minute. We know telepathy happens. We have valid experiment after experiment. Maybe your thoughts are reaching out to somewhere. Now I'm not ready to do an experiment on whether God is listening at the other end. Yet we are starting in an interesting direction. This is something we can discuss some other time but is of real importance. It is not all just curiosities and oddness.

Mishlove: You raised an interesting point in the 1972 original paper. You compared altered states of consciousness with Kuhn's idea of paradigms. This suggests that people can enter an altered state of consciousness where they can have an effect on a different paradigm.

That paradigm might be, for example, we are all connected. This would be versus what scientists typically believe in their normal consciousness: we are separate.

Tart: Yes. Again, I like the analogy of different tools. It's wonderful what you can learn about the world with a Swiss army knife. It is also wonderful what you could learn with a magnifying glass. I don't have any more tools within immediate reach here, or I might get carried away. But to know how each tool is useful, this [magnifying glass] makes a very bad hammer. If you've got to drive in nails, you're going to break it. So, with more tools, you learn more things. I love learning. It's so neat. I can remember when I was a little kid. I would wake up every morning, with an attitude. I can express it intellectually, but it was an emotional feeling too. It was, "Wow, another day. I wonder what's going to happen today!" Then, of course, I learned to be responsible, and began thinking about my troubles and responsibilities. I became normal. But I have managed to get a little bit of that "how interesting" back. It makes a big difference in life.

Mishlove: Charley Tart, this has been a fabulous discussion. We could talk for hours about these topics because they are so engaging. I hope we can do more of these interviews. For the time being, I think we have given our viewers a nice introduction to the issues involved for the psychenauts of the future.

Tart: If I have raised curiosity enough that someone wants to find out more, good. If I've outraged anybody with these outrageous ideas, good. Think about why they are so outrageous and what you know of the subject.

Mishlove: I'm looking forward to having the opportunity to discuss the other topic that has intrigued both of us. The relationship between parapsychology and spirituality.

Tart: Yes, right. All right.

Mishlove: We will return to that topic. Thank you, Charley.

Tart: Good to have a chance to share ideas.

Mishlove: It has been a true pleasure.

16

Spiritual Implications of Parapsychology

~

Recorded on November 20, 2018

Jeffrey Mishlove: Hello, I'm Jeffrey Mishlove. Today we will explore the spiritual significance of parapsychological phenomena. With me is Professor Charles Tart.

Welcome, Charley. It's a pleasure to be with you once again to explore the spiritual implications of parapsychological phenomena. I think an interesting place to start is with J.B. Rhine. Back in the 1960s when he left Duke University, Dr. Rhine set up an organization called the Foundation for Research on the Nature of Man. I think his intention was to use parapsychology data to establish human beings as having a spiritual nature.

Charles Tart: I think that was the case, yeah. And that scared a lot of people then. They figured we had a hard enough time being scientifically accepted, and if we have the slightest hint of spirituality or religion, the field of parapsychology would be labeled as consisting of a bunch of fanatics, not real scientists. There's a certain truth in that, but it goes to an extreme when we ignore the spiritual implications of this work.

Mishlove: I know there are parapsychologists today who get very uncomfortable when spirituality is brought up.

Tart: Some of them may be watching right now, in the future, and getting very uncomfortable.

Mishlove: Well, I hope so. I think it's good to make people uncomfortable from time to time.

Tart: I have a self-definition that will make it a little easier for them. I normally don't define myself as a parapsychologist. I define myself or describe myself as a transpersonal psychologist. I am interested in the spiritual: what it means, what makes it happen, things like that. From that broader perspective, parapsychology is a technical subspecialty and encompasses the reality or lack of aspects of spirituality.

Mishlove: I do think it is possible for somebody to be a complete materialist and to explore parapsychological phenomena, hoping that someday there will be an explanation for the data we now have and contained within existing metaphysical parameters.

Tart: I support those people all the way, if they don't say, "Do not look any other way. We have the only way that's going to work." Yet it hasn't worked or shown any definite signs of working. I'm a little bit cruel to my physicist, materialist friends on this parapsychological stuff. When they say there is a physical setting, I say, "Right, so then you'll not only understand the ESP and the like better, but you'll be also able to control it." Because to me that was the test of a good scientific theory. You can affect things more effectively and talk about it well. There is not a parapsychology experiment I know of, yet, that works better because we plugged Schrodinger's constant into Einstein's energy mass equation. It works better except for the psychological aspect. If you're a physicist, you have enormous psychological charisma. So, some of our best experimenters are physicists, but I think it's the psychological oomph they have, if you'll excuse my technical term.

Mishlove: I know that Ed May at SAIC, a physicist, did a lot of research on what he called the gradient of entropy as it pertains to remote viewing targets, a physical measure. He determined to his satisfaction that the higher the gradient of entropy, the better the target. People were able to zoom in on it, using remote viewing.

Tart: Yeah, I know that and I'm glad Ed did the research. But insofar as I understand what he is measuring, I think it translates almost completely into how interesting the target. A target that's got lots of interesting things has more entropy in the sense of physical changes in qualities. I don't know if that's been separated out from basic physical characteristics.

Mishlove: I'm not sure either. I did have the impression that sometimes what Ed May measures, as a gradient of entropy, is hardly visible to the human eye.

Tart: Maybe. I don't understand it that well to be able to comment. But I do want to follow up on this business of physicists having a lot of charisma, as it were, to make ESP happen better. I've known Russell Targ since the mid-1960s. I completed my postdoc work at Stanford and I've kind of kept up with Targ's interests. When he started talking about remote viewing work, I was very impressed. It looked like they were getting a lot more ESP coming from their percipients than we get in the usual kind of card guessing, the multiple choice guessing. Occasionally I would ask him or Hal Puthoff, "How do you do it? What's the psychological procedure whereby you create this very rich setting?" They would both look at me like, "Psychological procedure? What's that? We're physicists. We do an experiment."

Right then and there was a degree of confidence from the highest prestige branch of science that immediately said: okay, here's one component. It helps to be a much higher prestige scientist than, say, a psychologist or a sociologist and whatnot. Students even know the status levels involved here. When I first visited their lab at SRI, it was brought home to me what a wonderful psychological setting they have. First thing, SRI is a major think tank. You don't just wander in there. You've got to have an invitation. You get met at a desk where there is a security guard standing nearby. Then somebody who is on the inside must come down and vouch for you, while you get a name tag. You must be accompanied even to wander around the hall. I think it was Hal who came to get me and said, "Let's go up to our lab." We walked several hundred yards to their laboratories. He didn't just walk through the halls. He took short-cuts through some other people's labs. Oh, the equipment in those labs, the blinking lights, the oscilloscopes. I knew I was in a temple of big science.

Then he and Russ showed me some of their successful remote viewings, the drawings and the descriptions, and they're just so good. I'm thinking, wow, this is a lot better than the college sophomore in an ESP experiment asked to guess cards by a professor. They had a fantastic psychological setup at SRI, which they were completely oblivious to, and probably made it even more effective. They were not faking anything. They were just physicists doing an experiment.

Mishlove: There's a sense in which I would say scientists, and particularly physicists, are the high priests of our society.

Tart: Yes.

Mishlove: They have almost a religious aura around them. I don't know if I would call it spiritual, though.

Tart: No, but these are the priests who tell you what reality is. They know reality so well they can drop a nuclear weapon on you if you don't agree with them. That's impressive. I mean, physicists are incredibly brilliant. Of course, they're not looking at the spiritual side, but they've got the prestige.

Mishlove: I know Russell Targ very well and have for decades. I consider him a close friend. I know that early on in his career, before he entered college, he was an amateur magician and explored ESP. He was absolutely convinced. He has a mind like a steel trap. Once he made up his mind that ESP is real, it became a total focus on his part.

Tart: When Russell talks to you about it, he does it with this calm certainty of someone who knows rather than somebody who thinks "maybe" or "some data suggests." He's got it and he's a physicist. It's real.

Mishlove: It reminds me of a funny old comedy routine by a comedian named Lord Buckley. He jokes about Jesus and how people believed in Jesus. He said, using kind of hipster lingo, "When he lays it down, it stays there." I think Russell is that kind of a person.

Tart: Yeah. And of course, one of the major issues in parapsychology, which I've been trying to make my colleagues look at for 50 years, is the psychology of the experimenter. Some experimenters never get ESP out of their experiments. Others get it routinely. Why aren't we measuring the characteristics of the experimenter? We've got a little lore about this: certainty, facility and being friendly with people and whatnot, but no systematic look at it. I think it is derived from a desire to be accepted by mainstream science. We must show how objective we are with no characteristics. We are logical entities, observing and theorizing only. End of story. That's not how it works with people though.

Mishlove: No, because in effect, one of the main implications of parapsychology, and I think of quantum physics as well, is that this distinction that we make between subjective and objective is something of an illusion.

Tart: It's tricky, yes. I can't explain it any further than that. But this stuff does indeed remind me that our ideas of reality are handy for everyday going to the grocery store, but there is a lot they don't cover.

Mishlove: An interesting note: there are enormous spiritual implications from the data, and you have written about them extensively in a couple of your books. But one thing that puzzles me: is there a correlation between being a spiritual person and being very psychic. They seem to have orthogonal parameters.

Tart: Really?

Mishlove: Yeah. It seems to me you can be very psychic and not be very spiritual, I think. And you can be very spiritual and not be particularly psychic.

Tart: We've known people like that, but I would argue we have a smaller sample. We're talking about extreme people at one end or the other. It's complicated by the fact that in a lot of spiritual systems, there's an injunction that you're going to become more psychic as you become more enlightened. But don't mess with it. It will swell your ego and send you off on power trips. Leave it alone. If you must do anything with it, sneak it in. Don't let anybody know. This makes it very hard to discern spirituality. I don't know how to measure how spiritual people are, anyway. There are lots of conventional criteria, but I'm not sure how well they work. They are also easily faked. Some of the people making a good living as spiritual teachers have ethics and genuineness that is very questionable.

Mishlove: When I say people who are very spiritual, it has to do with the language they use, the food they eat, the clothing they wear. Those things are superficial.

Tart: Oh, yes. I sat on my zafu meditation cushion and ate only vegetarian for 10 days, as preparation for this interview.

Mishlove: And it shows. (laughs)

Tart: I'm sorry. I'm all for eating healthy. But as a psychologist, my main concern is the junk food of the mind that people eat and what it does to their thoughts. I suspect it has a lot bigger impact than what goes into their physical body. And let's make a distinction between religion and spirituality, because I think it's important for where we're liable to go in this discussion. When I say spiritual, I generally mean someone having a very powerful personal experience. They feel connected to all life, to the universe, to God, to other beings … something like that. They know the importance of connection and love and such things. It changes the way they live their life. They're now spiritual people, not so much because they're supposed to be, because, given the way they've experienced the world and hopefully continue to get glimpses of, it's the only sensible way to live. So, for instance, religion can tell you that you'd better be good to other people or you're going to go to hell. An enlightenment experience might give someone a taste of this idea: I'm not all by myself. I am connected to everybody. So, if somebody is suffering, I'm suffering at some level, too. So, I'm going to be considerate and nice to that person because it's the only sensible thing to do.

So, spirituality is more of an individual sort of thing. But then, of course, after somebody comes along with a spiritual experience, they get followers who organize committees, then have scholars develop doctrines to integrate with the lords and ladies, and the king, and how they run things. When you talk religion, you're talking more about social and psychological kinds of things, which is all right. I've tended to put it down, being a loner myself, but I realize we need religion to help foster social harmony. It's not the same thing as direct spiritual experience.

Mishlove: Do you equate spirituality with mysticism?

Tart: Equate is a strong word, Jeff. So, I would rather not say equate, but let's say they are highly correlated. When I talk about somebody having a spiritual experience, most of these could be described as a mystical experience, which means it's overwhelming and it usually changes the person's identity. They feel that who they are is now different. And it feels connected to the rest of life and is extremely difficult to describe in words. Part of the connotation of a mystic experience is, "Well, it was like, no, it wasn't like that. Well, no, it was like …" It reminds me of a joke Bob Monroe, of *Journeys Out of the Body* fame, once told me. It's a classic joke about a man who is driving in the country, trying to find a place. He gets totally lost. He finally sees a local and pulls over to ask how to get to his destination. The local says, "Oh, yeah, you take three crossroads down here, and then you see a red barn and you turn left. No, wait, that won't get you there. You should go back …" Finally, he says, "No, I'm sorry, you can't get there from here." You've just heard what amounts to a paranormal phenomenon. I have such a terrible memory for jokes, I usually never remember them. (laughs).

Mishlove: Well, you got that one. That was funny. But let me ask you this question. Would you regard spirituality or mysticism to be independent of belief systems? Or is there a correlation?

Tart: Yes and no. Your belief system is going to have a major effect on whether you're likely to have a mystical experience. So, for instance, some religions don't encourage mystical experiences. The founder of the religion and the saints had them long ago. Today you just follow the doctrine, and they say any experience will mislead you, versus something like Buddhism where we teach you how to meditate. And you can have the same kind of experience as the Buddha had or at least something on the way. It's possible for a belief system to either block you from having the experience or to help you get there. Then once you have it, if you try to share it with anybody, their belief system and your belief system start to interact. We're both from California. We can use words like "vibration" and "aura." We think we understand each other. Yet often there is a question as to how well. So, spirituality and mysticism are not necessarily correlated.

Let me give you an example. People often ask me; how did I get interested in parapsychology? I was raised as a Lutheran, as a child back in New Jersey, and my parents weren't religious. My mother knew what was right and wrong. My father wasn't interested, but my grandmother was deeply religious, and she went to church every Sunday. When I became old enough, she started taking me to Sunday school and then on to church. Grandmothers are the source of unconditional love. If it was good enough for her, it was good enough for me. So, I got involved in being a Lutheran.

Further on into my teenage years several things happened. One is that I became a teenager. And, like a teenager, I became very good at spotting the hypocrisy of adults. These people talked a good game about their religion, but I wasn't at all sure they lived that way. But even more, I was in love with science and read extensively. I'd go to the main city library and bring home several books on science each week. I found out very rapidly that science seemed to be saying, religion is nonsense. Not only is religion nonsense, but all religion is also nonsense. The very idea is preposterous. It's filled with crazy stuff. It became clear to me soon there was a lot of truth in that. There were some strange ideas in religion that seemed to go against fact. It didn't necessarily make people good, either.

I experienced a lot of conflict from this because, coming out of childhood, I was very devout. I prayed regularly. I wanted to be good.

But then my scientific side was developing, questioning. Was I just laying some kind of weird trip on myself? Then I discovered—I don't quite remember how, call it by accident, maybe Accident with a capital A—books on parapsychology. I thought, aha, you can use the method of science to check some of the ideas in religion and spirituality. Take the idea of prayer, for instance. From the viewpoint of common sense or ordinary materialistic science, prayer is talking to yourself. If you talk out loud, your prayer will travel 10 or 20 feet before it gets lost in the noise of the environment. And that's the end of it. If you're praying internally, it doesn't even go that far. So, it's talking to yourself.

So maybe it's good to talk to yourself. It helps you work some things out. It can certainly work that way. Maybe it just multiplies your craziness. But then, I think, there are these experiments in telepathy from J.B. Rhine and his colleagues, that many people have done. You've got somebody at one place trying to send an image or something similar, and somebody totally shielded materially at another place, making a record of what comes through. They get it right enough of the time that it is not chance. Well, wait a minute. Prayer then is about telepathy? Is it about being able to send some information or a desire beyond your actual physical location and being? That's interesting. What else could you begin to check about ideas in religion?

Then I discovered that historically, the Society for Psychical Research founded in 1882, was very interested in this question. Science was revolutionizing society, seeming to throw out all religion. A lot of people said, "yes, science has got a lot going for it." and it's obviously true, but are we going to throw all religion out? What's the basis for morality or decency? They were very interested. Can you apply the relative objectivity of science to religious mystical phenomena to find out what is true? That question inspired me. Basically, it is what my life has been about professionally. Can I use basic scientific methods to find out more about phenomena that have spiritual and religious implications? And it's been interesting.

Mishlove: And so, in many ways, that's the project of transpersonal psychology, and by extension, parapsychology.

Tart: Almost, but not quite. That's how I would define transpersonal psychology: looking into the reality of mystical and spiritual phenomena. But most transpersonal psychologists I've known simply take the reality for granted. They know these kinds of experiences are generally good for people. So, it's a question of how do you teach people to have these experiences? This doesn't have much impact on mainstream science. They argue that transpersonal psychology is a lot of nuts in California who believe anything. It's all right as they are relatively harmless and whatnot. I've often suggested that in transpersonal psychology we need to check the basic reality of these phenomena. I suppose there are times when training one to have a powerful illusion, one that's good for you, is a good idea. By and large, I'd like our spiritual ideas to be based on as much reality as we can check out. Not that we may be able to check out everything, but we can check out some things.

Mishlove: Recently I've interviewed a fellow named Jorge Ferrer, who is a transpersonal psychologist. He considers himself a member of the second wave of transpersonal psychology.

Tart: Oh, that makes me feel old.

Mishlove: He defines the first wave of thinkers, people like yourself and Stan Grof, as sort of having laid out a vision. It is consistent with what Aldous Huxley called the perennial philosophy. But Ferrer says there's a real problem. If you take that point of view, you're basically identifying with the idea that all is one: a philosophy of Advaita Vedanta. There is no division, no duality. But Jorge says, there are many spiritual traditions that don't subscribe to that view. He goes on to say, it is not proper for a transpersonal psychologist, without evidence, to elevate any one tradition over any other.

Tart: I'd go along with that. Transpersonal psychology is a very new field of psychology. It's been around for 30-40 years, maybe, at the most. Sometimes the idea that all is one, that we're intimately connected, does reflect the kinds of experiences some people have and has positive effects on people. But I won't say that any one view is necessarily *the* correct view. I find truth in just about everybody's view about almost everything. I also find that almost everybody who's got a view that picks up some of this truth is liable to say, "Actually, I've got all the truth." Well, slow down. Humility, remember? It's supposed to be good to [have] humility. There's so much we don't know yet. If we're all one, how come we feel separate? That's an interesting question.

Mishlove: It is a very interesting question. I've heard some interesting answers to it. How would you address that?

Tart: I have no idea. But that's an interesting question. Here's one way I'd think about it if you told me, I've got this new mystical technique. If you practice it for a couple of days, you'll have the experience of feeling at one with everything. The universe is perfect, and everything is going as it should. You'll never have to do any practice or anything again. It'll last all the rest of your life. Part of me would say, yeah, oh boy, no more suffering, no more worry. Another part of me would say, might this get a little boring after a while? I like to solve problems. Maybe one of the reasons for human life being what it's like is that it helps us to evolve. You don't train somebody to be stronger, for instance, without having them lift heavier and heavier weights. So, one mystical vision I've seen people talk about is that this is a training school. Souls incarnate here. It's a very tough course. If you can master this, you're very useful in the rest of the cosmos, much more than the people who stay in kindergarten.

I'm remembering an experience Bob Monroe described in one of his out-of-the-body trips, after experiencing them for many years. Early on, he'd had a mystical experience of the classical kind. I can't remember it exactly, but he found himself in some place with colored clouds moving and evolving with incredible beauty. Music like you wouldn't believe was playing. It was so calm and ecstatic at the same time. The experience ended, and for years he kept thinking, oh, I wish I could go back to that place. Well, many years later, he did go back. And after a while, he noticed, didn't this cloud sequence go that way before? It's looping. It's a repetition. He had an insight. He'd found his way into a spiritual nursery, which was good for calming disturbed souls or baby souls or something like that, but you didn't want to remain forever and ever and ever. So, I would like to be able to vacation at the resort you describe. But I also like to feel I'm doing something useful, not just feeling blissfully happy all the time.

Mishlove: Well, when it comes to parapsychological data—

Tart: Well, wait, I want to add to this idea. I realize to some people who are suffering a lot in life, my comments may sound like a snotty sort of thing to say. I realize there are many people who are suffering, terribly. I'm lucky that I don't have much suffering. So, if I can contribute to understanding our minds better, to help people become happier and more competent, that's important. An actual accomplishment there, not just feeling good myself, is my priority.

Mishlove: I think the main claim of Buddhism, for example, is that this is a path that leads you to end suffering.

Tart: Which is quite a claim. I've been a student of Buddhism for 30-40 years now, something like that. Should I say, "Oh, God," when I'm talking about Buddhism? Anyway, sometimes I hear it expressed as you reach a state of enlightenment, forever beyond any suffering, or maybe you no longer exist in a form that suffers. It gets very hard to describe, in other words. I'm a little suspicious of that. I know Buddhism can give you tools for not suffering and for being more effective in what you do. But I think when you use those tools, you can help other people. You help with understanding and so forth. So, I'm not a Buddhist. I never call myself a Buddhist. I am a student of Buddhism [and] a student of various other spiritual traditions. I don't know enough, or believe simply enough, to fit into any of those slots.

Mishlove: My sense of the people I know in the field of parapsychology is that they're mostly like you. They're eager to study various religious traditions and spiritual paths, but they're not particularly joiners. If they join anything, it's their commitment to the scientific method.

Tart: That reminds me of what you mentioned about first wave and second wave transpersonal psychologists. That might be partly an artifact of that. If you got into transpersonal psychology 30-40 years ago, you were a misfit or a rebel. You were bucking the common trend then. The emphasis was doing it on your own. Maybe that's not the case as much anymore. Where have I read that in some cities there are more yoga studios than coffee shops? I find that hard to believe, but wow.

Mishlove: I've lived in Las Vegas and in Albuquerque; not necessarily either city is known as a great spiritual center, but there are yoga studios all over the place.

Tart: I have a cartoon on my refrigerator that shows the road into Las Vegas and a big billboard that says, "Las Vegas, a faith-based community."

Mishlove: One of the main interests, since the field of psychical research was formed in 1882, is to answer the question of whether human beings survive the death of the physical body. There is some component of consciousness that is not dependent on the physical body. This seems to me to be very much related to the issue of spiritual implications in our field.

Tart: Yes, very much so. For a long time, people had an awful lot of misery in their lives that you couldn't do anything about. I'm thinking, for instance, [that in] a culture I imagine ancient India to have been, there wasn't much social change, as you went along. On a minor scale, somebody might—No, they didn't even change caste very much. So, the idea of reincarnation there, and the possibility that you might in the next life have a better situation in life, could be appealing. Or it might be a horrible idea: I've got to carry out garbage in this life and the next life and the next life and the next life. When we think about reincarnation in the West, I think we tend to see it as an opportunity for progress. But the idea of some kind of survival does add a dimension of meaning to life.

In 2009, when I published my book, *The End of Materialism*, now in paperback with a strange new title of, *The Secret Science of The Soul*. I am sure they're going to come and take my white lab coat away for daring to use the word "soul." But anyway, the idea that there was meaning in life, it didn't just end. You are born, you eat, you suffer, you die; end of story. But that you may go on and somehow help to reduce suffering, now, that's a very tricky idea. Because, of course, it helps the ruling class keep us peasants down and from a revolt. So, pie in the sky. When science began showing that a lot of religion seemed to be full of nonsensical ideas, the idea of survival went out of fashion, too. Your mind is just a function of a physical brain, all the chemicals exchanging with the little electrical junctions and so forth. That's all there is to it. So obviously when you die, and that stops happening, and no more you.

Now, if you've lived a very miserable life, that scenario is appealing. It means no more suffering. I also have an interesting twist to it. I think the evidence is good enough that we may survive in some form. I'm not sure. In the book, I talked about the five things that I thought we had enough evidence to be sure of, things like telepathy. Also, a bunch of things I called "the many maybes," where there was enough evidence to think these may be real, but we're not quite sure yet. Some kind of survival after death was one of those many maybes. I think the evidence is quite exciting sometimes. At other times you see wish fulfillment and projection and longing to avoid the reality of death affecting the way people see things. So, I don't know. Of course, if we survive death, at some point I'm going to find out if I was right in thinking it's possible. If we don't survive death, I'm never going to be embarrassed for thinking that because I won't be embarrassed about anything or feel anything or think anything. I'll be gone. I can't buy these old ideas that some cruel God is going to punish me for all eternity because I didn't sing enough hymns. That's just too, too primitive.

To me then, it is very important to try to get evidence on, "do we survive?" One of the things that's surprised me about this subject is how few people seem to be interested in the evidence. My naïve thought, for instance, was of course that any organized religious group would love to hear about this evidence. They all assume some kind of survival. But the degree to which religious groups have asked, come and talk to us, is almost zero. I think it may be that the question is so vital to them, and they've already invested so much in believing they're going to go to heaven or similar, or unfortunately go to hell, that they don't want any questions asked. It's all right if science says people who attend church live three years longer, on the average. But that is even tricky because it involves asking some questions. I think a lot of religious beliefs do not want you to ask questions.

I can understand where that is coming from. I suspect there are areas of my life that I don't want anybody to ask questions about. I may have covered them up so well that I don't know what they are. And I think I'm very open minded, but who knows? Science has progressed in the material world so much because it keeps asking questions. Yes, it is obvious that a heavier object would fall faster than a light object, except when you start checking it out. No, they fall at the same rate. Okay, we've got a new invisible force called gravity and whatnot. Science progresses by asking questions. I try to ask the questions. I hope they'll come up with answers that I think are conducive to human welfare. But sometimes, I don't know.

Mishlove: Do you think in theory that it's possible to answer that question of survival?

Tart: I think, in theory, it is to get a more certain answer than we have now. But I'm not at all sure whether we can get any absolute answers. We can talk about the odds. We might say, given what we know now, the odds are 50-50, whether we survive. But if we perform that kind of research and it comes out in a certain way, the odds might now increase to 70-30. I think we must live a lot of our life based on playing the odds. We don't have any certainty of one sort or another as to how our life will go. I live as if I may survive death; the way I am and behave will have long-term consequences. That sounds too noble somehow, but I'm just an old boy scout. I'm trustworthy, courteous, and kind. If there is something like karma, if the qualities we develop in this life go into an afterlife or reincarnate, that is worth knowing about.

Mishlove: And of course, you know the University of Virginia has a database of well over a thousand cases of young children remembering past lives. They've been able to research and locate the family where some of these past lives were lived.

Tart: That's very impressive. One of the things that got me very educated about parapsychological research happened while I was a student at MIT. I thought I was going to be an electrical engineer. I was browsing in the bookstore one day among the books-on-sale table, where books that didn't sell you could buy for a dollar, and that fit within my budget. I saw a book called *The Search for Bridey Murphy*, which I immediately started skimming over. I thought it must be some novel, then I noted something about hypnosis. Well, I'm interested in hypnosis. As you know, and some listeners probably know, it was about a man named Morey Bernstein who hypnotized a housewife in Colorado. When he took her back in time through hypnosis, she started speaking with an Irish accent. She claimed she once lived as Bridey Murphy in Cork, Ireland. Then she came up with several interesting facts about Cork as well as a few things that couldn't be checked one way or the other. Unfortunately, there simply weren't many records and some things were probably wrong. But hey, if I asked you what you ate for breakfast one year ago, on this very day, you'd probably get it wrong, too.

I knew a lot about hypnosis by that time and much about parapsychology because I am a reading addict. I thought the book wasn't bad. The author did not make excessive claims. He said simply, this is the evidence. It would certainly be interesting if we reincarnate, and you could pick up memories through hypnosis. Then the book hit the bestseller list, somehow—it hadn't belonged on the throwaway book table—and people went nuts. It even included a book being published shortly after titled, *A Scientific Report on the Search for Bridey Murphy. It included* chapters by a few physicians and psychiatrists who, I knew, were authorities in the field of hypnosis. These critics knocked the book badly saying Bernstein made this awful, nonsensical claim.

I got very puzzled because these were real scientists and highly respected. I didn't remember Bernstein in *The Search for Bridey Murphy* book making those types of claims. I went back and reread the book. They were denouncing him for things he never said. I said, "Oh wow, even if you're a scientist, some topics like reincarnation can get you so upset that you start ranting and raving and making a fool of yourself. Wow." I've noticed that kind of bias in science, also. Materialism is not just scientific fact. It's a belief system. It is a belief system that's very comforting, in a lot of ways. So, for instance, when I was young and got sick sometimes and I was still conventionally religious, I often wondered, have I been bad? Is God punishing me for sin? Now we know so much about medicine, I say, "Oh, I've got the flu. I'm not bad." What a relief to put it down to a simple physical cause like that. So, you can get invested in total materialism and actively push the spiritual away because it raises questions about how you live your life. All these factors interfere with trying to get clearer scientific knowledge about the spiritual, but we have yet to work them out.

Mishlove: I had the opposite reaction to those scientists. I first encountered *The Search for Bridey Murphy* in third grade.

Tart: Third grade?

Mishlove: 1956.

Tart: You were precocious.

Mishlove: My classmate Lee Rosenthal gave a book report on *The Search for Bridey Murphy*. He said, "I'm reading this book and it shows that we have lived before." At that moment—I remember it vividly sitting at my little desk—I experienced chills running up and down my spine. I mean, tingling strong, like what we might describe today as a kundalini experience.

Tart: Really?

Mishlove: Yeah.

Tart: Was the feeling like you were angry or relieved that this was the case?

Mishlove: It was like an acknowledgement that there is something true here. Something I'd never heard before. My whole body just resonated. It was quite physical.

Tart: Well, it was quite a lesson in the fact that our culture was not ready for the idea of reincarnation. Really, the vitriol. I've seen it in my own career, too. I'm still getting criticized sometimes for studies I wrote up 50 years ago and "Tart claimed this awful thing." No, I said the opposite. Why don't you read what I said, if you want to criticize me?

Mishlove: It's very risky for someone in a scientific profession to make a claim of a spiritual nature. You're likely to get pounced on.

Tart: Yep. You and I know that.

Mishlove: Yet it does seem to me the data of parapsychology has spiritual implications. You talked about telepathy earlier. What we're talking about with telepathy, clairvoyance, precognition, and retrocognition, is the ability of the human mind, now well documented in hundreds of experiments, to reach out beyond the range of the nervous system itself—and its ability to obtain information from distant locations, both in space and time. It suggests, minimally speaking, space and time are not obstacles to the human mind.

Tart: Yes. Under ordinary circumstances, I think I'm here, right? I have a boundary. My skin and I only have direct contact with stuff through my physical senses. That's fine for 99.9% of what I do. Our human senses are extremely good at picking up what's in our environment. We hear things; we see things; we smell things. We can act adaptively to protect our bodies. But all the parapsychological data says, wait a minute. We may be focused here 99.99% of the time, but don't say our ultimate nature is limited to here. It goes way beyond that, in some sense. Most of the time it's fine. If I'm trying to think of what to say to you now, I don't want to telepathically pick up what somebody in China is thinking as they cram for a test somewhere. That would be distracting. But the parapsychological stuff gives us a direct taste sometimes of, oh, I am more than that.

Let's take remote viewing, for instance. When they were first doing the remote viewing research at SRI, there were enough parapsychologists in the San Francisco Bay Area that, for a year or two, I held a meeting at my house once a month. These active parapsychologists talked with one another about what they were doing. Very early on, Russell Targ and Hal Puthoff came to talk about their remote viewing sessions. It was still brand-new stuff. They described these impressive cases and, well, yeah, they seemed to get awfully good outcomes, yet stuff doesn't generally work that well. Then they said, now we will show you how it's done. "Okay, Hal is going to go away. In a half hour, we're going to ask each one of you to close your eyes and try to get pictures of where he is located." Okay, I didn't expect anything to come of it. We had no idea where Hal went. A half-hour drive from my home, that narrows it down to a million places. No point trying to guess at the spot.

Time came; Russell was there. He asked us to look for pictures and so forth. I didn't get much mental imagery. My mind was busy thinking, as it usually is. But finally, I had one mental image that was good. I thought for a few seconds I was looking into some factory. It was a factory that had a lot of white machines with wheels or parts that went around in big circles. It was very brightly lit. Then the image was gone. It didn't make any sense to me. So, I wrote down a little description of it and so forth.

Hal eventually came back, and we all got in some cars. He drove us to where he'd been, in front of a laundromat. At first, I was looking at the street and my image didn't look anything like it. Then I turned and investigated the laundromat window, to see white washers and dryers spinning around under the bright, fluorescent lights. "Oh, it happened to me. Wow." Experiences like that carry a lot of weight. This is one of the important things about parapsychological phenomena. They can take some spiritual ideas and make them something that's an actual experience, not just an abstract sort of idea.

Out-of-body experiences are another example. I read many accounts of people who had out-of-body experiences where they found themselves floating to the ceiling. They viewed their body down below, and the like. The experience might only last half a minute. But especially interesting is the aftereffects. For almost all these people, they would say something like, "I do not believe I am going to survive physical death. I *know* I'm going to survive physical death. I've been alive and conscious outside my physical body." It might not affect us strongly, hearing of another's experience, but it brought home to these experiencers: there is something in me that might survive death. They could be wrong. But this is a bit of evidence saying, yeah, that's stacking the odds a little in its favor.

Mishlove: I think it was Einstein, I could be wrong, who said that the most important question anyone can ask is, "Is the universe friendly?"

Tart: I hope so. I don't know. It doesn't seem very friendly sometimes when we have wildfires and the like, but I hope so.

Mishlove: Yes, you're suffering right now in the Bay Area. I understand the air quality is terrible there.

Tart: Oh, yeah. They've told us not to go outside for the next few days. It's awful.

Mishlove: My gosh. I know that takes us away from our planned topic, but I couldn't help thinking about it, because there you are, close to those biggest fires ever in California.

Tart: But of course. We the voters have rationally made bond efforts for major reservoirs and the like to increase our water supply. We think ahead, right? You must distinguish fantasy from fact when it comes to everything in life, including parapsychology, including Einstein also. I used to have some great Einstein quotes, which I found people often made up. There's a whole industry of making up ideas attributed to Einstein.

Mishlove: William James, as well. There are William James quotes I have never been able to validate. But about the data of parapsychology, it does suggest to me telepathy, out-of-body experiences, remote viewing, and all suggest that time and space and consciousness are not what we conventionally assume them to be. There is sort of the standard Western creed, I think you call it in one of your books. We are nothing more than the molecules and cells that we are made of.

Tart: Exactly. That creed, incidentally, is an exercise. I make people quite unhappy with it when I have them do it as an exercise. It takes straightforward ideas about everything as only material and puts them in a form like a religious creed. One that people recite together. It's a real bummer when they discover they believe a lot of stuff simply because it's in the air around us. And, in my life, there is no inherent meaning to this universe. My life has no inherent meaning. I'm not going to quote more of the Creed here, because I don't want to give your viewers a bummer, too. But for someone who would like to find out something about beliefs you have, and may not know you have, but which affect you, I recommend that chapter in the *End of Materialism* book. Or what's the name of the paperback, Jeffrey?

Mishlove: *The Secret Science of the Soul.*

Tart: There you go.

Mishlove: But it does seem to me—and I think you point this out—there is something comforting about that belief. It's like I don't have any illusions. I'm facing reality, bleak as it may be.

Tart: About 95% of the people who have done the exercise, in my workshops, find it very depressing. But they are glad they're now wiser.

They discover they have built-in resistances. About 5% say, "Yeah, no worry about whether I'm moral or immoral or whether I'm going to hell or not. I'm just a bunch of chemicals sloshing around. You can't blame me for anything. Blame my parents or my genes or my chemistry," or something like that. That doesn't make for a deep value system.

Mishlove: Then there are people who might take the parapsychological data and say, yes, this data shows us there is what some philosophers name a supersensible world. A world beyond normal consciousness. But then they add, we don't know if it's a friendly supersensible world or if it might be a hostile world. There could be harmful forces out there; entities we would rather not know about.

Tart: Right. I'd rather not know about them. I will admit, this is one of my biases. I find ordinary human beings, you and me and our friends and everybody, are quite nasty enough, without any unusual kind of help. I know this is a bias on my part. I'm not inclined to test it. For instance, can you hex somebody to kill them? I am not about to initiate any experiments along those lines. I'll tell you a funny story instead. It goes back to talking about the power of belief. An anthropologist I know visited South America. He was talking to a group of shamans about hexing people to death. They asked, "How do Westerners explain it?" He explained to them the psychosomatic theory. Stating it gets you so stressed out that it stresses your body badly and you die. Then, he couldn't understand why the group of shamans practically laid on the floor laughing. They explained, "You Westerners, how can you be so dumb? If somebody knows they have been hexed, they get a shaman to fight the curse off. It must be totally unknown for it to work." Belief systems.

Mishlove: I do know of at least one report in the anthropological literature of a person hexed by a shaman who resided in a different country and didn't know of the hex, who died. So, I mean, the negative potential of all of this. In fact, interestingly, Charley, I interviewed a scholar of religion, Jeffrey Kripal, who is also a member of the Parapsychological Association. He points out, when we think of religion, of God, oftentimes religions exist to protect the congregation from the awesome power and fear of God. I mean, if you read the Bible, he points out, if you see God, you will die. Even in our most comforting religions, God is horrible, awesome, so powerful, much like a nuclear reactor.

Tart: Oh, yes. There have been times in my life when I've wanted to have some kind of mystical experience that would make everything right. I sort of say a prayer for that, and then I add, "Incidentally, God, could you sort of manifest gradually in a non-threatening form so that you don't scare the hell out of me?" I know there is that possibility. I recognize my bias against it. There are areas in life in which I can be intellectually open and other areas in which I know I can't handle it. Precognition, for instance. I know the evidence that sometimes we can get information from the future that is overwhelmingly positive. That's one of the five things we can be sure of exists. But it makes absolutely no sense to me. I try not to think about it.

Should I try not to think about it in the future? If I have some sense of humor about it, I'm not too worried. There may be psychic entities that can be nasty. I hope not. But I could say the same thing about human beings. I wish that no human beings were nasty, but we have some horrible examples. I know a little bit about helping people be a little bit "gooder." And I think, as a transpersonal psychologist, we can train people to have the kind of mystical experiences that connect them with the universe., I think we can improve the state of the world this way. But I'm not into pushing at the other side of it. And, of course, people manipulate the hell out of other people by scaring them about demons and evil spirits and so forth. So that gets tricky.

Mishlove: It does. Let me just bounce off you, before we end, one other statement that Jeffrey Kripal recently made when I spoke with him. He said he's sick of people saying, "We shouldn't use the term paranormal, that it's normal." He said, "No, it's not normal." And he's looking at extreme examples like his collaboration with Whitley Strieber, a UFO contactee. He says that when you look at these extreme examples of the paranormal, there's nothing normal about them at all.

Tart: Well, this is all a matter of how you define normal. Words that should just be descriptive often take on emotional values. The term remote viewing, for instance, was deliberately used instead of saying "we're doing clairvoyance experiments at SRI," because clairvoyance is weird woo-woo stuff. It shouldn't happen and doesn't happen and yet drives you crazy. But remote viewing, that sounds like an engineering application. SRI then does engineering applications. Parapsychologists approximately every five to ten years get all worked up over, we've got to change the name of the field because parapsychology has got the wrong associations. Nobody ever comes up with anything better. Some people talk about anomalies or anomalistic phenomena. The people who are frightened by and try to suppress parapsychology, still know what you're talking about. There is a lot of irrational opposition to parapsychological research, as you know.

Mishlove: It's likely to remain no matter what name we use.

Tart: But I think we need lots and lots of it. Let's face it, parapsychological research is such a tiny amount of scientific research; it's almost as if it doesn't exist. It's only because we've been doing it for a hundred years that we've got enough of a database to be able to say things like telepathy happens, for sure. But in terms of transpersonal psychology identifying as bigger than what's in your brain, we need to know how much of it is real and how much isn't. If you feel at one with all the entities in the universe, would you do better on a clairvoyance test? Or is that feeling something that might be valuable in and of itself. Doesn't it mean you connect to something? Interesting questions.

Mishlove: Very important questions to me. I hope in the coming decades, we see some answers.

Tart: Yes.

Mishlove: Well, Charley, this has been a fascinating conversation. I'm delighted we have this time together and I can share this conversation with our viewers. Thank you so much for being with me.

Tart: Thank you for holding these conversations, Jeff. You bring the stuff out.

Mishlove: I look forward to having more with you in the future.

Jeff in 2023

About the Author

~

*N*ew *Thinking Allowed* host, Jeffrey Mishlove, PhD, is author of *The Roots of Consciousness, Psi Development Systems, The PK Man,* and the *New Thinking Allowed Dialogues* series: *Is There Life After Death? UFOs and UAP: Are we Really Alone?* and *Russell Targ: Ninety Years of Remote Viewing, ESP, and Timeless Awareness.*

He is the recipient of the only doctoral diploma in the world from an accredited university that says, "Parapsychology." It was awarded from the University of California, Berkeley, in 1980. He is also the Grand Prize winner of the Bigelow Institute essay competition regarding postmortem survival of human consciousness.

Index

~

Index

Jung, Carl Gustav, 94, 141, 156

K

Kammann, Richard, 91–92
Kardec, Allen, 180
Kripal, Jeffrey, 205–206
Kundalini, 153–154, 201

L

LaBerge, Stephen, 144
Learning to Use Extrasensory Perception (book), 41, 63, 73, 75, 77, 79, 81, 83, 85, 137, 159
Leary, Timothy, 171
Life After Life (book), 174–175
Living the Mindful Life
Love, 11, 64, 75, 82, 98, 114, 118, 123, 126, 128, 130, 132, 134–135, 150–151, 155–157, 170, 172, 177, 185, 192–193, 199
LSD, 171
lucid dreams, 143–144, 147
Lutheran, 11, 130, 193

M

Magallón, Linda Lane, 181
Marijuana, 6, 10, 138, 144
Marine World, 182
Marks, David F., 91–92
Marxism, 18
Maslow, Abraham, 150
May, Edwin C., 188-189, 90-91
May, Rollo, 151
Maya, 54
McMoneagle, Joe, 82
MDMA, 172
Meditation, 2, 5–6, 18–19, 21, 47–48, 56–61, 69, 109, 115–116, 120, 131, 152–153, 159–165, 167–168, 173–174, 176–177, 191

Meetings with Remarkable Men, 108–109, 112
Mescaline, 171, 181
Mind at Large (book), 85
Mind Science: Meditation Training for Practical People, (book), 159
Mindfulness, 6, 53, 55–62, 116, 157, 159–161, 167
MIT, 8, 66, 98, 200
Monastery, 21, 57, 108, 172
Moody, Raymond, 174–175
Monroe, Robert, 148, 179–180, 192, 196
Morris, Freda, 182
Moses, 154
Mutual Dreaming, 142, 181
mutual hypnosis, 139, 181–182
mysticism, 151, 192–193

N

National Oceanographic and Aeronautic Administration, 48
Nature, (journal), 91
nervous system, 47, 50, 104, 184, 202
neurophysicalism, 125
New Age, 155

O

On Being Stoned, (book), 10, 137
Open Mind, Discriminating Mind, (book), 107, 137
Ornstein, Robert, 6, 10, 140
Ouspensky, Peter Demyanovich, 109–110
out-of-body experience, 7, 10, 147, 152, 179, 203–204
Owens, Ted, 155

Index

www.ingramcontent.com/pod-product-compliance
Lightning Source LLC
Chambersburg PA
CBHW031429270326
41930CB00007B/633